Out of the Frying Pan

D0111583

Out of the Frying Pan

Reflections of a Japanese American

by

Bill Hosokawa

University Press of Colorado

Published by the University Press of Colorado
P.O. Box 849
Niwot, Colorado 80544

All rights reserved.
Printed in the United States of America.

The University Press of Colorado is a cooperative publishing enterprise supported, in part, by Adams State College, Colorado State University, Fort Lewis College, Mesa State College, Metropolitan State
College of Denver, University of Colorado, University of Northern Colorado, University of Southern Colorado, and Western State College of
Colorado.

The paper used in this publication meets the minimum requirements
of the American National Standard for Information Sciences—
Permanence of Paper for Printed Library Materials. ANSI
Z39.48-1984

Library of Congress Cataloging-in-Publication Data

Hosokawa, Bill.
    Out of the frying pan : reflections of a Japanese American / Bill
Hosokawa.
        p. cm.
    ISBN 0-87081-500-8 (alk. paper). — ISBN 0-87081-513-X (pbk. :
alk. paper)
    1. Hosokawa, Bill. 2. Japanese Americans—Biography. 3. Japanese
Americans—Social conditions. 4. Japanese Americans—Evacuation and
relocation, 1942–1945. 5. Japanese Americans—Cultural
assimilation. 6. Japanese Americans—Ethnic identity. 7. United
States—Race relations. I. Title
E184.J3H622   1998
305.8956073'092—dc21
    [B]   98-26215
                                                              CIP

07 06 05 04 03 02 01 00 99 98   10 9 8 7 6 5 4 3 2 1

Contents

To Alice

Foreword

T hrough vividly recollected personal experiences, Bill Hosokawa, this country's leading journalist of Japanese descent, provides a fresh and moving account of the greatest injustice in twentieth-century U.S. history, describing how he, his wife, their infant child, and tens of thousands of other Japanese Americans were herded into U.S. detention camps during World War II.

Ignoring the Constitution, the U.S. government rounded up these innocent people and locked them away based solely on race. The fact that they were American citizens, and guilty of no crime, did not matter. Japanese Americans on the West Coast were taken from their homes and businesses to inland camps, including Heart Mountain Camp in Wyoming, where the Hosokawas were incarcerated.

This abruptly ended Bill's budding journalism career. After graduating from the University of Washington in his hometown of Seattle, he had gained prominence as a writer and editor for the *Singapore Herald,* the *Shanghai Times,* and the *Far Eastern Review.* It was this newspaper experience that helped him win his freedom from the Heart Mountain camp. *The Register* in Des Moines, Iowa, offered him a job and Hosokawa spent three years in the Midwest. After the war, Hosokawa found a job with the *Denver Post,* which had been notorious for criticizing "Jap"-lovers and blasting the concentration camps for "coddling" the "Yellow

Menace." At the *Post,* he rose through the ranks as copy desk chief, makeup editor, wire services editor, executive news editor, assistant managing editor, Sunday editor, editor of the *Sunday Empire Magazine,* associate editor, and editor of the editorial page. After his retirement, the *Post*'s archenemy, the *Rocky Mountain News,* hired Bill as their readers' representative.

Hosokawa wrote the definitive history of the *Denver Post,* entitled *Thunder in the Rockies* (Morrow, 1976), and *Nisei* (Morrow, 1969), the story of second-generation Japanese Americans, as well as seven other books. A former president of the American Association of Sunday and Feature Editors, the Colorado Authors' League, and the founding president of the Colorado Freedom of Information Council, Bill taught journalism at the University of Colorado, the University of Northern Colorado, and the University of Wyoming and received an honorary doctorate in humane letters from the University of Denver.

The *Denver Post* and Historic Denver, Inc., honored Hosokawa as one of 100 Coloradans who have made a lasting impression on the state and its residents. He has been not only a sharp reporter and editorial commentator, but also an active participant in Colorado affairs since 1946. Bill has been inducted into the Denver Press Club Hall of Fame and the National Cowboy Museum Hall of Fame. In addition to freelancing for national magazines such as the *Saturday Evening Post* and *Reader's Digest,* he has been writing a weekly column since 1942 for the Japanese American Citizens League newspaper, *Pacific Citizen.* A selection of some recent columns makes up half of this volume.

Hosokawa has served as Japan's honorary consul general for Colorado since 1974 and received the Order of the Rising Sun from the Japanese government for promoting U.S.–Japanese understanding and trade. His broad contacts, passionate concern, alert intelligence, and activist participation make this autobiography rewarding reading from many perspectives.

This quiet, unassuming man has made a tremendous difference through his lucid writing and heroic efforts to right wrongs. After many years of reflection and firsthand experience in so much of what he writes about, Bill Hosokawa eloquently and thoughtfully captures in this book the bittersweet Japanese American experience.

Incidentally, Hosokawa is the only person I know who is quoted in Webster's Third New International Dictionary as an authority on the use of a particular word. That word is, well, let H. Allen Smith, the humor writer tell you about it. In a letter dated June 10, 1970, Smith wrote to Hosokawa:

Dear Bill:

Today I was sitting here slaving away on some piece of writing when suddenly I wanted to use the word funk in a sentence. As I do once every five minutes, I whirled my chair around and checked in Webster Three, which is always at my elbow. . . . And there is ole Bill Hosokawa reigning as one of several top authorities on funk the noun. P. 922.

I must add that one day not long ago I was looking up tripe. Cited as an expert was a guy I know, Stephen Longstreet of Beverly Hills. I couldn't let him know about it; somehow it wouldn't sound right to advise him that he is top authority on tripe.

It seems all right, however, to tell you how high you stand on funk, if not funking.

Not entirely willing to take Smith's word, I checked Webster Three. There was Hosokawa on page 922, cited along with the likes of Sinclair Lewis, Paul Gallico, *Nation,* and the *New Yorker*. Hosokawa said he had used the word to describe a depressed state of mind in an article for the *Saturday Evening Post.*

There is no place for funk in this book except in this introduction.

Indulge me one more paragraph. Hosokawa is among notables profiled in the Newseum, a museum of the history of the news profession, in Arlington, Virginia.

—Tom Noel
Denver, Colorado

Out of the Frying Pan

Chapter One

To Singapore and Back

On the day I was dragged, reluctant and apprehensive, to a kindergarten class at the old Main Street School in Seattle, the only language I understood was Japanese. English was so foreign to my ears that I hardly knew my newly acquired first name. Until a few days earlier, it had been Kumpei, an uncommon Japanese name translating roughly as "meritorious peace." But after consulting friends, my father added the solidly Anglo-Saxon William to help my teacher cope with the problems of introducing me to the American educational system. My ignorance of English was so complete that I didn't even know how to say I needed to go to the bathroom. As a result, when the class stood up and straggled out for recess, my knickers were damp and I left behind a small puddle on the floor.

Main Street School was on Sixth Avenue between Jackson and Main, in the center of what passed as the business section for Seattle's Japanese immigrants, who made their living from small retail stores, barbershops, restaurants, and a pool hall or two. Shortly after I became a kindergartner—it must have been about 1920—the entire student body marched off to occupy the spanking new Bailey Gatzert School, which the Board of Education had erected a mile or so away. The redoubtable Ada J. Mahon was principal, presiding over a student body that was approximately 98 percent Japanese American. The old Main Street

School was converted into a Chinese restaurant called the Golden Pheasant. Or maybe it was the Golden Dragon; after some seventy-five years, it's hard to be sure.

Most of my fellow kindergartners were as ignorant of English as I. We spoke Japanese at home and to each other. The reason is obvious: our parents didn't want to contaminate us with their halting English. Yet they felt it was imperative that their children, born in the United States as I was and thereby anointed with U.S. citizenship, should be educated as Americans.

My father and mother and I—and later a little brother—lived with several other Japanese immigrant families in a rickety tenement rooming house perched on a steep hill above Main Street. Timbers anchored the building to the clay hillside, which became very unstable after each of Seattle's frequent rains. A more diligent city building department would have condemned it long before we took up residence.

The apartment building, if it can be dignified with the term, was called the Sanraisu. What that meant I did not know, but years later I realized it was a corruption of "sunrise." I also learned that what my folks referred to as *neru* was flannel, which my mother sewed into nightclothes, *donguri pantsu* were dungaree pants, *hanboku stekki,* which we enjoyed on rare occasions, was hamburger steak, and, of course, *oh rai* was "all right."

My kindergarten experience was brief. Before long, we moved into rented rooms in a less geologically precarious area near Sixteenth Avenue and Yesler Way, where cable cars plied their leisurely route between downtown and Lake Washington. On the corner was a small grocery store, redolent of kosher dill pickles, run by the Glickman family, which was made up of papa and mama—neither of whom spoke any more English than my folks did—and five American-born kids: Louie, Bessie, Sadie, Edith, and Harry. They all lived in a tiny house attached to the store.

I soon discovered that with a penny coaxed from my parents, I could buy a little wax bottle that contained a few drops of sweet red syrup. After the syrup was gone, the wax could be chewed like gum. And if I could resist the wax bottles long enough, Mr. Glickman would give me a heaping vanilla ice cream cone in exchange for five pennies.

Harry Glickman, who was about my age, became my friend and mentor. He taught me that peanut butter, despite its repulsive appearance, was delicious when spread on bread, that hazelnuts and wild black-berries, which grew in empty lots, were edible if one waited until they were ripe, and that the little black water beetles in the wading pool at City Park were harmless even though the kids called them bloodsuck-ers. In return, I told him we Japanese liked to eat the wild fiddlehead ferns that poked up through the grass in the spring, but I am not sure he believed me.

Later in my boyhood, my friends and I would walk a mile or so to Chinatown, which adjoined Japantown. There, for a quarter, we could get an abalone that had been sun-dried until it was as hard as oak, the color of saddle leather, and shaped like a hockey puck, only slightly smaller. We called it *bongui,* which must have been reasonably close to its real name because the Chinese shopkeepers understood us. We would shave off small slices with a pocketknife and suck and chew on them, enjoying what we considered to be an exquisite flavor. A *bongui* gave us pleasure for weeks.

Once, at Washington School, which I now attended, my second-grade teacher Miss Waughop asked if I had ever been tardy. I did not know the meaning of *tardy* and didn't have the wit to ask. So, taking a chance, I held up one finger, and it went into the record book that way, although I was always prompt.

Somehow, I began to absorb English. My classmates were mostly Jewish—kids with names like Max Stalinsky, the Katz brothers, the Cohens, the Israels, and Bennie Kaddaner, whose family ran a bakery. There was Jake Steinberg, who changed his name to Jack after he be-came an attorney, and the very smart Betty Selznick and Alice Reznick. There were also gentiles of various origins, like Adolph and Orlo Spaetig, Donald MacDougal and his sister Grace, and Nick and John Koblykovich. By the time they reached high school, the Koblykoviches had short-ened their name to Koblyk. On Jewish high holy days, only a handful of gentiles—of whom I was one—showed up for classes, and the teachers left us pretty much to our own devices.

As I began to solve the mysteries of English, I excelled in other subjects. Eventually, I was awarded the role of George Washington in a school play about the travail at Valley Forge. Some parents in our com-munity, cosmopolitan as it was, weren't quite ready to accept a "Jap boy" as the general who would become the father of his country. The principal quietly quashed this outbreak of petty racism, which I did not hear about until some time later.

It was during this period that an uncle made the mistake of leasing a small strawberry farm near the town of Kingston, across Puget Sound from Seattle. Strawberry culture requires an enormous investment of backbreaking stoop labor. My mother took her younger son, Ritsuro—later called Robert—who was nearly four years my junior, and went to help her brother grow berries. I was left at home with my father because I was enrolled in school. Each day he fixed a simple brown-bag lunch and prepared my breakfast before he went to work. He was quite capable in the kitchen, having cooked semi-professionally early in his American career, but day after day he fed me nothing but a soft-boiled egg, toast, and a glass of lukewarm milk for breakfast. I have shunned soft-boiled eggs ever since and don't even like them hard-boiled. Perhaps that is why, at my advanced age, my cholesterol count is reassuringly low.

My father started life in America in 1899 as a sixteen-year-old immigrant railroad section hand somewhere in Montana. One day he got into an argument with the foreman, quit his job in a huff, and, though he knew nothing about American geography, rode freight cars west to Sacramento, California. There he became a schoolboy, meaning he hired out as a live-in domestic while attending grade school with white children half his age. Later he worked as a migrant farm laborer, following the harvest up and down California. He also made several voyages to the Philippines as a mess boy on an American military transport.

By the time he settled in Seattle, he was running an employment agency. He had a little office, a telephone, and a place where job seekers could sit and play Japanese board games—*shogi,* which is like chess, and *go,* a very complicated game of strategy—while waiting for work. Well-to-do white women would call in to ask for a "day worker" to wash windows, beat rugs, mop the kitchen, polish the varnished woodwork, and take on other heavy chores. My father would parcel out these jobs and collect a small commission. His English was adequate for this kind of service, and he commanded a certain status among the Japanese immigrants because he dealt in white-collar work.

About 1913, more than a dozen years after he came to America, he returned to Japan to find a bride. The woman selected for him was Kimiyo

Omura, younger daughter of the headman of a village near his. She probably had little to say about the match, because in those days marriages were arranged by the parents and a go-between. Pictures of my father at that time show a dapper, mustachioed young man in a bowler hat and rimless glasses. He must have been considered quite a catch. But I have never understood how he persuaded his bride to accompany him across the Pacific to an uncertain life in a foreign country with a strange language and unfamiliar customs. Additionally, she was somewhat above him socially. He was the son of a peasant farmer and had only a grade school education. She had completed middle school—unusual for women at that time—and had been an elementary teacher for several years.

My mother was a gentle woman. I don't recall that she ever raised her voice or her hand against me. But my brother was spanked once when he threw some baked sweet potatoes, which were considered a delicacy, on the floor. After he grew up, he enjoyed embarrassing his mother by reminding her of that act of violence. When my father bought a secondhand Star touring car, she decided she should learn to drive, an unusual ambition for women in those days. She was still a novice when she ran a stop light. My brother and I, who were in the car, immediately raised such a fuss that she never drove again. When we were young, she worked late into the night at the kitchen table, stringing beads for an importer to supplement the family income. Later, she recalled the lessons of her youth and taught Japanese cultural arts such as flower arranging and the tea ceremony to Japanese American women.

One day I discovered the Yesler branch of the Seattle Public Library. There I became acquainted with the works of Edgar Rice Burroughs, creator of Tarzan, the lost son of Lord Greystoke, who had been rescued by the Great Apes in darkest Africa and reared by them into a man of remarkable strength and talents. I also got to know Joseph Altscheler's fearless frontiersman, Henry Ware. The heroic Ware was a deadly shot and very adept at foiling savage Indians who were guilty of nothing more than protecting their property in the wilderness that would become Kentucky. These novels taught me the pleasure of reading and helped improve my command of English, and I became a regular library patron.

If there were books about Miyamoto Musashi, Benkei, and other Japanese warrior heroes, who I learned about from my parents, I did not encounter them. What I did find was a fascinating volume about the first creature to discover that oysters were not only edible but very tasty when eaten alive fresh out of the sea. This creature, according to the book, was Probably Arboreal. I thought it a delightful name.

My parents encouraged my reading, but they were also concerned that my understanding of Japanese was rudimentary. They enrolled me in the local Japanese-language school, where classes were held every weekday afternoon from 3:30 to 5:30. During this time, my Jewish friends were out playing ball or, in season, eating wild blackberries and cracking hazelnuts.

Enrollment at the Japanese school was composed largely of other unhappy youngsters who couldn't see the wisdom of extending their school day by two hours. With such lack of enthusiasm, there wasn't much learning taking place. Largely disregarded were the urgings of parents who worried at the prospect of taking illiterate children to meet grandparents on a visit to the Japanese homeland someday.

Under the laws then in effect, my parents, immigrants from Asia, could not become naturalized Americans. That privilege was extended only to Europeans. And as Asians, they were subject to discriminatory laws that applied only to "aliens ineligible to citizenship." For example, they could not own real estate. For a time, we rented the upper floor of a house owned by an Italian immigrant family who lived downstairs. Mr. d'Avonzo made his living shoveling gravel for a paving contractor and spoke even less English than my father, but because he was not an alien ineligible to citizenship, he could own property. Years later, when my father wearied of buying houses for others with his rent payments, he bought a modest home in my brother's name, because Robert, though a minor, was a citizen by birth. This was a common and usually accepted piece of subterfuge.

Denial of citizenship must have troubled my mother. For several years while her children were growing up, she enrolled in naturalization classes so that she would be ready if the laws were changed. She even tutored European immigrants who were about to take the citizenship exams. Nonetheless, the Americanization of my parents was a slow and difficult process, as was their effort to introduce me and my brother to Japanese language and culture. Their English did not improve, mainly because they had very little contact with English-speakers. My brother and I learned rudimentary Japanese, a very difficult language under any circumstances, and we conversed—communicated would be too ambitious a word—with our parents in a strange mixture of English nouns and Japanese verbs. I suspect our lack of progress could be blamed in part on our resentment at being under Japanese influence in an American world. I did not learn to speak Japanese reasonably well until I reached adulthood.

Though my parents were rather unsuccessful in teaching us about Japan and the Japanese, they insisted we be good students in English. Their assistance came mainly in the form of moral support, because they understood very little of what we were studying, other than arithmetic. They encouraged us to study hard, to develop a curiosity about everything around us. They even subscribed to the daily newspapers for our benefit, though our interest was limited at first to the comics. They rejoiced when our grades were good, rewarding A's with small sums of money to be saved for a college fund, and urged us to study harder when our marks dropped a little.

Even as I struggled with English lessons, memorized the Pledge of Allegiance, and adopted the legend of George Washington and the cherry tree and the Gettysburg Address as part of my American heritage, I was also aware of the Japanese family background that made me different from my classmates. Of Japan, however, I knew next to nothing. It was a distant place, somewhere beyond a vast ocean, where my grandparents lived. It was also a rather fearful place. My mother sometimes told me, particularly when I toyed with my food, of the hunger that often stalked that land. And from that I learned frugality.

Occasionally, when my father was angered by my indolence or disobedience, I was threatened with being sent to Japan to live with the grandparents I had never met. This was not an entirely idle threat. A few of my Japanese American acquaintances had suddenly disappeared. Later, I learned they had been sent to Japan to be reared by relatives while their parents struggled to make a living in the United States. I assumed my grandparents were kindly people, but the fear of being sent away led me to modify my behavior, at least for a while.

Two other guidelines frequently invoked by my parents helped govern my deportment: *Hito ni warawareru*—you will be laughed at by others—and *Sonna koto wo shitara haji wo kaku*—such actions will cause disgrace. This deference to the opinions of one's peers led to a certain conformity of behavior on my part until one day I staged a quiet teenage rebellion, vowing to myself that I would live my own life, regardless of community or peer pressures. Perhaps that was the day I became fully Americanized.

Still, I was not unaware that pressures based on racial differences existed. I heard my parents talking about *haiseki*—the social and economic discrimination they encountered because they were Japanese. I heard them discussing the Ku Klux Klan, which was still active in the Deep South, terrorizing blacks and threatening Catholics in many parts of the country. I felt compassion for the blacks and not entirely naively wondered if the Japanese would someday be made a target of the Klan's hate.

(As a teenager I played on a basketball team in the city Parks Department league. Our center was a rangy and amiable black youngster named Brennan King, who went on to become an outstanding high school coach. All the rest of us were short little Japanese who scurried like terriers around him. We lost about as often as we won.)

At home, I learned the virtues of hard work, honesty, humility, obedience, loyalty, respect for parents, and love of learning. These traditional Japanese values were highly prized by my parents, and their values became mine. Yet I felt I was also an American, entitled to claim America's values, as well as its history and traditions. This is not to say I resented the Japanese part of my heritage; rather, at this stage of adolescence, my attitude toward the Asian portion of my heritage was, for the most part, passive.

Far more thoroughly than others realized, I was shaped in thought and action by the American school system, testament to its capacity for molding the offspring of immigrants, whatever their port of embarkation, to the American image. Though I was the product of centuries of breeding in a world alien to the West, I approached adulthood with an American mind, albeit one fortified by many Japanese values. It was my Japanese face that could not be changed.

In January 1929, at age fourteen, I entered Garfield High School as a freshman, and the following summer, I was ready for a job (child labor laws were still years in the future). Despite some misgivings on my mother's part, I signed up with some friends to work in a salmon cannery in Alaska. Even at fourteen, I wasn't the youngest hired. My friend Sam Kozu was only twelve, and several others were just thirteen.

Asians had been working as laborers in the salmon canneries since the turn of the twentieth century. First came the Chinese immigrants, then the young Japanese. As the Japanese grew older and found steadier employment, they were replaced by kids like us and Filipino migrant workers who spent their summers in Alaska and their winters in California on vegetable and fruit ranches. Contractors, representing the cannery owners, recruited the laborers, transported and fed us, supervised the cannery operations, and paid the wages.

Most of the contractors were Japanese, which made it easy to get a job. Because we were earning adult pay, we youngsters were treated like adults from the very beginning. Before we embarked, we were given a rudimentary physical examination that consisted of standing before a federal health service inspector, unbuttoning our pants, and displaying our penises to show that we were free of venereal disease.

The most intense shock hit us when we boarded a small coastal liner for the voyage to Alaska. Our steerage quarters were down several decks, just above the waterline, in a dimly lit hold that reeked with the sour smell of tobacco smoke and vomit. Canvas slings hung in four tiers served as bunks. The lowest were suspended only a few inches above the grimy steel deck. The air around the upper bunks was hot and fetid. There must have been sixty or seventy of us packed into the hold—Japanese Americans like ourselves, elderly Chinese, Japanese bachelors, young Filipinos—all bound for various canneries. There were usually a number of card games going on. We youngsters spent most of our time on the foredeck with nothing much to do except watch the seagulls trailing the ship and return the stares of the first-class passengers on the upper deck.

We knew we wouldn't be eating the type of meals that passengers on ocean liners were served, but the food was far worse than we expected. Our first meal consisted of sausage stuffed with gristly mystery meat, boiled potatoes, bread, and coffee. The sausage was passed in galvanized iron buckets around the long tables where we sat family-style and served ourselves. The best—or possibly the worst—part of it was that the sausages were plentiful. The next meal was hash, and the quality of food deteriorated from there. It was a relief to reach our cannery, located in a picturesque and isolated cove called Hidden Inlet, after two-and-a-half days aboard ship.

The wilderness settlement consisted of the cannery, a warehouse, a bunkhouse for whites and another for the Asians, and the superintendent's house on a slope overlooking the area. All of the structures except for the superintendent's house were built over the water on pilings. Heavily wooded hills rose abruptly behind this outpost, and our only escape on days off was at low tide, when we could go exploring along the beach.

Some jobs required more stamina than skill, like standing at a trough hour after hour cleaning gutted fish under a stream of icy water. Understandably, the fellows who drew this duty were called slimers. The fish were first beheaded and slit open by a huge machine called the Iron Chink, which clearly indicates who did this work before the machine was invented. Other assignments included feeding an endless stream of gutted salmon into a noisy machine that stuffed one-pound chunks into cans that were then capped automatically and sent into a retort to be cooked with live steam. The luckier kids—somehow I was one of them—worked in the warehouse labeling the cans, packing them into wooden cases, and stacking the cases until they could be shipped out.

Our compensation consisted of sleeping space in the bunkhouse, board, and wages of $75 a month for ten hours of work six days a week, Monday through Saturday. Any work in excess of sixty hours a week was paid overtime at $.25 an hour. My check for the summer's labor was less than $160. My parents told me to bank it for college, but many of my friends turned over their earnings to their parents to help feed the family.

We youngsters were called "guarantee boys" because we were guaranteed two months of work during the canning season. The "season boys" opened the cannery in the spring and closed it down in late summer after the salmon were gone. No one was paid until he returned to Seattle. That was just as well, because there was no way to spend money except on gambling with each other.

The whites worked mostly as machinists and supervisors, while the Asians performed coolie labor, and this distinction carried over beyond the workplace. Every week or ten days, a ship would arrive to drop mail and food supplies and pick up the cases of canned salmon. I could not help but notice that if five sides of beef were unloaded, four would go to the white bunkhouse and one to ours, even though we outnumbered the whites substantially. They ate steak, roasts, and stew. Our diet consisted mostly of salmon, three times a day, served with rice, boiled greens, and soybean soup. There is nothing more tasty than fresh red salmon lightly salted and grilled. But three times a day, day after day, was a bit much. Why was salmon served so regularly? Because it cost the contractor nothing.

Vegetables grew wondrously well during the long summer daylight hours of coastal Alaska. But there was another reason why our greens were exceptional. In the outhouse, jutting out over the water at the back of our quarters, galvanized sheet iron troughs served as urinals, draining into five-gallon tin buckets. We provided a virtually endless supply of liquid fertilizer for the cook, whose job included tending Chinese cabbage and other greens in a little garden carved out of a nearby hillside.

There was one other source of food. The contractor would ship a half dozen or so baby pigs with the season boys. The pigs were kept in a pen behind the bunkhouse, where they grew rapidly on table scraps. By midsummer, they were ready for butchering. The Filipinos in our crew, who were accustomed to butchering livestock in their villages back home, were happy to take on this responsibility, anticipating welcome relief from the steady diet of salmon. After hearing the pigs squeal in terror before they died, I could never enjoy the meat that appeared on our table.

Most of the salmon brought to the cannery had been trapped. A trap was a barrier of log piling jutting out from shore into a salmon migration route. When the salmon encountered this barrier, they would swim into a holding pen that had no exit. Every few days, a tender—a small boat—would visit a series of traps owned by the cannery, dipping out the catch and delivering the fish to be processed. By noting how deeply the tender rode in the water as it approached the cannery, we could estimate the number of fish it carried. If the vessel rode low, it could be bringing in as many as 25,000 salmon, which meant eighteen to twenty hours of nonstop canning, except for meals and brief coffee breaks. The catch had to be processed without delay because the following day, more fish would arrive.

I returned to Seattle in time to start school. Nationwide, the Great Depression was settling in, and the next summer, a guarantee boy's pay was reduced to $35 a month. I did not return to Alaska for seven years.

By the spring of 1932, after three-and-a-half years, I had earned enough credits to graduate from high school but had the option of returning for a final semester, during which I would be eligible to take part in sports. So I returned to Garfield High, motivated by a burning desire to play on the varsity football team. This was an unrealistic ambition because I weighed less than 140 pounds after lunch and was the kind of aspiring athlete about whom coaches said, "He isn't very big but, boy, is he slow!" As usual, I didn't play enough to win a varsity letter.

Because I already had enough credits to graduate, I saw little point in exerting my intellect on academic subjects. I therefore spent most of my time in the machine and electrical shops. And on journalism. I soon discovered that serving as sports editor on the school weekly was more fun than running a lathe or working out algebraic equations. Though engineering was a popular career choice at the time, I decided to study journalism at the University of Washington, a state-supported school where the tuition was nominal, and forget about building dams and bridges or designing airplanes. My parents simply assumed I would go on to college. What the heck, jobs were hard to get for a high school grad.

Tuition at the university, where I enrolled in the fall of 1933, didn't amount to much, maybe $20 to $25 per quarter, with books costing about as much. I was living at home and working afternoons and nights at the *Japanese American Courier,* a four-page weekly published by Jimmie Sakamoto, a former prize-fighter who had been blinded by ring injuries. Today, Jimmie would be called a community activist; back then, he was preaching militant, unquestioning loyalty to the United States to second-generation Japanese Americans, the offspring of immigrant parents, and trying desperately to keep his newspaper solvent. The Japanese word for second-generation is *Nisei.* The word is short enough to fit nicely into a headline, but Jimmie would not allow it, maintaining that it was foreign, and American-born children of Japanese immigrants should be identified properly as second-generation Americans. Try fitting "second-generation" into a one-column headline.

I had no salary, but when the time came to pay my tuition, Jimmie's wife Misao, the business manager, would somehow find enough money for me. This precarious arrangement left me little time or cash for other activities, particularly on campus, so I returned to Alaska in the summer of 1936 to get my finances in order. Wages had increased somewhat due to a militant union movement, and I needed more money than the $10 a week I had been earning during the summer at a wholesale produce market unloading vegetables from farm trucks in the predawn darkness and reloading them into grocers' vans. This was a job that required only a strong back and enough intelligence to know the difference between tomatoes and potatoes.

During this period, the Roosevelt administration invented what was called the National Recovery Act (NRA), a bundle of hastily conceived regulations designed to revive the economy. At markets like the one I worked at before returning to Alaska, NRA rules specified that vegetables could not be sold for less than a government-mandated minimum price. It was an attempt to override the market's supply-and-demand pressures and guarantee the farmer a certain return for his produce even if it couldn't be sold. If produce remained unsold, as it often did, it was condemned and dumped after it was no longer marketable, and the federal government would compensate the farmer for his loss. Day after day, crates of spoiled lettuce, spinach, celery, cucumbers, tomatoes, cantaloupes, and other perishables were hauled to the dump. On the other side of the railroad tracks was a Hooverville where hundreds of unemployed men lived in shacks made of carton boxes and old sheet metal. They ate whatever they could scrounge. The vegetables piling up in the market would have been a godsend. But NRA said surplus produce could not be disposed of until it was no longer fit for human consumption. Federal inspectors prohibited us from giving it away while it was still edible, even though they knew it would never sell. In time, I would encounter other similarly stupid government regulations.

I came back from Alaska in the fall of 1936 with nearly $200, enough to see me through my junior year at university, where my studies in journalism were going well. I had high hopes for the future, but it didn't take long for reality to raise its ugly head. One day my journalism faculty advisor called me into his office. "Why do you want to continue studying journalism?" he asked after a few preliminaries. I replied that it appeared to be an interesting way to make a living. "Well," he said, "let me be frank. I don't think there's a newspaper publisher in the country who would hire a Japanese boy. You'll never find a job. It's not fair, but that's the reality. We can't encourage you to stay in the journalism school and we can't kick you out while your grades are up, but frankly you would be smart to transfer into the business school or find something else."

He knew what he was talking about. When my classmates were assigned to work on newspapers around the state during spring break, I was left behind. "Afraid you wouldn't be welcome," my faculty advisor said when I protested. Many years later, after I had attained an executive position in the *Denver Post* newsroom, this professor invited me back to the University of Washington to speak at a conference for high school seniors interested in newspapering. The theme was opportunities in journalism. I accepted. I think it was his way of apologizing for how I had been treated, though he could not force himself to say so directly.

There were two other Asians in my class, and they received the same advice I did. One was Ed Luke, a bright, personable Chinese American. He eventually tied on a printer's apron and worked in the back shop of a movie industry weekly in Hollywood, where his brother, Keye Luke, had gained some notoriety playing Charlie Chan's eldest son. The other was Shin Kobayashi, who I thought had more writing talent than most of his classmates. After graduation he took a job with an English-language news service in Japan. Shin was stuck there during the war and was killed in one of the Tokyo firebombing air raids that took more lives than the atomic bomb at Hiroshima.

I got my sheepskin in 1937 and became the first Hosokawa with a college degree. (My brother has since earned a master's degree and a Phi Beta Kappa key, and my children have a doctorate and three master's degrees among them.) Although I had harbored no delusions, I discovered quickly that my professor had been right about professional opportunities. I went to work for $75 a month at the only job I could find—as a secretary at the Japanese consulate in Seattle. My job was to write letters and speeches for the consul, a career diplomat named Issaku Okamoto who was soon transferred to Singapore. My speeches must have been pretty good; at his farewell banquet, he

choked up and had to wipe his eyes while reading a particularly sentimental passage I had written.

Some months later, Okamoto sent word that a Japanese publisher
in Singapore was planning to launch an English-language newspaper
and was looking for an editor trained in the American style of journalism. Would I be interested?

I had only a vague idea of where Singapore was and what it was like,
but this seemed like a dream opportunity. There was one problem. A
short time earlier, on the promise of a raise in salary to $85 at the consu-
late, I had asked a fetching young lady named Alice Miyake from Portland, Oregon, to marry me. And she, in her innocence, had accepted.

Would Alice want to go to Singapore as my bride? Would we be
wiser to put off marriage until I came home in two or three years? Or
should we just call off the engagement? She opted for marriage and
Singapore. We were married in the fall of 1938 in a modest Methodist
ceremony in Portland, much to my father's chagrin. He would have preferred to underwrite a fancy wedding in Seattle, inviting his many friends
to an elaborate banquet that would have cost him far more than he could
afford; this was the old-country custom, particularly important when a
family's first son was being married. I wounded my father—and made
him lose face in the community—when I insisted a big wedding would
be an unwise and ostentatious waste of money.

My prospective employer paid our passage to Singapore, and Alice
and I enjoyed a leisurely honeymoon voyage that started in San Francisco, with stops at Honolulu, Tokyo, Kobe, Shanghai, Keelung in Taiwan, Hong Kong, and Saigon in what was then French Indochina. I was
seasick most of the way. Each time we visited a port, I was struck anew
by how large Asia was, and how greatly the cultures varied from country to country. I noticed how poor they seemed when compared to the
United States—even to someone like me, who had enjoyed but a modest lifestyle in Seattle.

My boss in Singapore turned out to be an easygoing, somewhat
vague middle-aged Japanese named Shohei Nagao. In a dingy office, he
published a Japanese-language daily that circulated among expatriates
and businessmen in Malaysia, Java, and Sumatra. He had somehow come
up with the idea of starting a newspaper for English-speaking Indians,
Chinese, and Malays who took a dim view of the British-owned dailies.
Whatever their merits, these papers were well established, and launch-

ing a competitive newspaper from scratch was a daunting challenge. But I had asked for it.

Nagao had only a hazy idea of what was involved in starting up an English-language newspaper and told me to undertake the necessary steps. That meant selecting type and ordering typesetting machinery, developing a prototype, assembling and training a staff, picking a name for the paper (the *Singapore Herald*) that all elements of the polyglot population could pronounce, setting editorial policy, and learning everything I could about Singapore's history, government, economy, business, and culture, as well as the idiosyncrasies of the various ethnic groups that made up the population.

Early on, I learned a valuable lesson about Singapore publishing tactics. There was huge interest in Joe Louis, the young American heavyweight boxing champ, and one day we received an early news flash saying he had knocked out challenger Tony Galento in four rounds. This was before the days the public had instant electronic access to the news. We put the story at the top of the front page. To help sell papers, it was the practice to print posters hawking the day's most sensational story in large black type, displaying them around town wherever we had newsboys. I ordered a poster that told the whole story: "Louis KOs Galento." Loh Kee Tek, our wizened little circulation director, protested strenuously. "No, no, no. How do you expect to sell papers if you tell the people who won the fight? What you gotta say is, 'Joe Louis Fight Results.' You gotta tease 'em into buying the paper." Of course, he was right.

There were other things I didn't know about newspaper publishing—selling advertising, building up circulation, paying bills—and I was glad they were Nagao's problems. Editing the paper posed enough headaches. One of my first major tasks was finding a wire service to provide the *Herald* with world news that was not already available in the other publications. The three major Singapore papers were served by Reuters, which is a British service, and American-owned United Press. To make ourselves unique, the *Herald* needed something different. The Hearst-owned International News Service had a local representative, Mr. Bannerjee, and I took my business to him. Within days after we started publication, INS canceled our contract. A satisfactory explanation was not forthcoming, but the hand of the internal security section of the British colonial government was evident. After that, the Herald was forced to rely mainly on the less-than-adequate Japanese Domei English news service delivered by radio.

The British security service's concern was understandable. With the Japanese military running roughshod over China, what was Britain to make of a Japanese publisher in one of its colonies starting an English-language newspaper edited by an American with a Japanese name? Whatever Nagao's problems with British officials might have been, I had only one encounter with them. It occurred after the outbreak of war in Europe in September 1939. One of my assistants, intent on finishing his assignment quickly so he could hurry off to slake his thirst, read only the first few paragraphs of a background story we picked up out of the *English Mainichi,* published in Japan, before okaying it to run in the *Herald*'s feature section. The story started innocuously enough, but the tone of the latter portion, which he hadn't bothered to read, was unmistakably pro-Nazi.

The British security officer who summoned me to his office wanted to know what the hell was going on. I apologized. He indicated that another treasonous mistake might result in revocation of my residence permit—meaning deportation—and suspension of the *Herald*'s publishing license. I told him I understood. After all, I was a guest in one of his country's colonies.

Newspapering even under those conditions was exciting for me. But it wasn't quite as much fun for Alice. My hours were long, and the only relief from tropical heat and humidity was going to an air-conditioned movie theater or nightclub. There was only so much shopping and sightseeing she could do on her own. One night she became horribly ill after a curried shrimp dinner. Shortly after that, she told me she was pregnant, didn't want to take a chance with local medical facilities, and wanted to go back to the States for our child's birth. Singapore today is a modern city, one of the world's cleanest. But back then, it was a typical tropical Asian settlement teeming with filth, odors, and germs.

I had no problem with leaving Singapore. We'd been there a year and a half, and the newspaper was growing. It was nearly time for me either to commit myself to a semipermanent stay, which wasn't entirely appealing, or move on. But if I returned to the United States, what could I do? I had become familiar with only a small corner of the vast and complex Far East and couldn't pass myself off as an Asia expert. And if I went home, would I ever be able to come back to places like Japan and China? Alice and I had many discussions. Ultimately, we agreed she would return to the States alone, have the baby, and live with her mother. Meanwhile, for one year, I would pursue opportunities in Japan or Shanghai.

We left Singapore in May 1940 just Hitler's armies were knifing swiftly through Belgium, the Netherlands, Luxembourg, and what was left of France, leading to the humiliating British retreat from Dunkirk. It appeared that if the United States were to go to war, it would be in Europe, not Asia, despite growing tension with Japan. Even so, I had many apprehensions about remaining in Asia. I would be thousands of miles away when I became a father. At the *Herald,* I had been paid an adequate salary in Singapore dollars, but when they were exchanged for U.S. currency, our savings were less than $1,000. I gave almost all of it to Alice, wondering how I would make enough to continue supporting her.

I traveled with Alice as far as Yokohama, where she boarded a ship bound for Seattle. In Japan I found English-language newspapermen were in demand. I was offered several jobs that paid much more than I had been making in Singapore. But I turned them down to go to Shanghai, where my old mentor, Issaku Okamoto, now the Japanese representative on the multinational Municipal Council that governed the International Settlement, had offered to make some introductions.

I wangled a travel pass from the giant South Manchurian Railway, which wasn't difficult, obtained a commitment from a weekly magazine in Tokyo to publish accounts of my impressions, and set off for Shanghai on a roundabout course. It took me from western Japan across the Korean Strait to Pusan, Korea. After a stop in Seoul, I went on to Mukden, Hsinking, and Harbin (where some 35,000 White Russian refugees had settled) in Manchuria, then back to Dairen, where I took a ferry to Tientsin, the port of Peking (now Beijing). There were many Britons in Tientsin, and Japanese undercover agents had come up with a weird idea for forcing them to leave. They organized what they called the North China Branch of the Irish Republican Army, which threatened violence unless the British went home. It was a ridiculous ploy but an indication of what the Japanese were capable of as they sought to dominate the East Asian mainland. From Peking, whose splendor from the imperial days astonished and delighted me, I took a train across North China to

Nanking and then down along the Yangtze River to teeming, bustling Shanghai.

Most of my travels wound through Japanese-occupied territory, and I began to realize the extent to which Japan had committed itself to taking over the mainland. Following their armies, Japanese carpetbaggers and their families were everywhere, establishing colonies and setting up businesses as soon as the "bandits"—the Japanese term for Chinese guerrillas—were "pacified," a nice word for "eliminated." U.S. policy was to persuade the Japanese to leave China and let the Chinese straighten out their own admittedly chaotic affairs. But Washington was being totally unrealistic. Even then it was obvious to a casual visitor that the Japanese were prepared to stay, and gentle persuasion wasn't going to work.

At the time, Shanghai had four English-language dailies. The *North China Daily Mail* was British-owned, looked like a British paper with classified advertisements on page one, and presented the British viewpoint. The *China Press* was Chinese-owned and reflected views of the Nationalist government. The *Evening Post and Mercury* was owned by an American insurance tycoon, C. V. Starr, and its militant U.S.-style news coverage irked the Japanese army, which had occupied the area of Shanghai called Hongkew. The fourth paper was the *Shanghai Times,* owned by an English expatriate named E. V. Nottingham but inclined to be quite tolerant of Japanese military excesses.

I found part-time jobs with Nottingham's *Times* and with Charlie Laval, an American who published a monthly business magazine called the *Far Eastern Review.* Laval had been in China for decades, and when things were slow, he enjoyed sharing his memories with me. He was a good teacher. Once I wrote a piece critical of Western imperialism, citing what had been widely reported as fact—that there was a sign outside a public park along the Bund in the International Settlement that said dogs and Chinese were not allowed to use it. Laval told me emphatically that I was incorrect. If I had bothered to check it out, he said, I would have found there were two signs, not one. I went to see for myself. He was right. One sign prohibited dogs, and the other prohibited Chinese. These signs individually were quite different from a single sign prohibiting both dogs and Chinese, thereby lumping the two together, and the nuances were important.

Many years later, I heard a veteran editor tell a reporter that assumption is the mother of all errors. "Check it out," he said. "Never assume anything. If your mother says she loves you, check it out." It was a lesson I had learned from Charlie Laval early in my career.

I had been in Shanghai several months when a cable reached me from Portland, Oregon. Alice reported the arrival of our son, Michael, and that all was well. I did not see Mike until he was more than a year old.

Shanghai was an exciting place in late 1940 and early 1941. The Japanese military, headquartered in the Hongkew sector, made threatening gestures almost daily toward the International Settlement. Japanese sentries on Garden Bridge, which connected the two areas, were arrogant and insulting. Refugees from the Japanese-occupied countryside had jammed the city. Grimy beggars, pickpockets, and prostitutes crowded Nanking Road, which was lined with well-stocked department stores, neon-lit restaurants, and shops displaying exquisite antiques. In contrast to tawdry Hongkew, which was full of Japanese carpetbaggers, the tree-lined streets of the International Settlement's French Concession maintained a quiet elegance. On the outskirts, gambling casinos, nightclubs, and jai alai frontons prospered, undoubtedly paying liberally for Japanese military protection. Oddly enough, the pleasure palaces were off limits to ordinary Japanese; such places were considered bad for their morals.

The international tension was palpable. Soon after I arrived in Shanghai, the U.S. consulate urged all unessential American personnel to leave, and American warships visited Shanghai less frequently. Many businessmen sent their families to the Philippines. One day I watched two Scottish regiments, which had been stationed in the International Settlement, march to the waterfront, bagpipes skirling, and sail away.

Spokesmen for the Japanese Foreign Ministry, army, and navy held a weekly joint press conference. Not much news was disseminated, but representatives of the news agencies—Associated Press, United Press, and the International News Service—as well as correspondents for French, British, and Australian news organizations showed up, in no small measure because the drinks and hors d'oeuvres were free. There was usually good-natured bantering between the correspondents and the spokesmen because both sides knew they were merely playing roles.

There was so much to do that my time flew quickly. About once a week, some Japanese American friends—bachelors or husbands separated temporarily from their wives—gathered for an evening of small-stakes poker and reminiscing about life in the States. Occasionally, I would go to the Seamen's YMCA for an American-style meal or to Jimmy's Kitchen, which advertised that its tables were scrubbed regularly with Lever Brothers soap, for its famous chicken noodle soup, hamburger steak, mashed potatoes, and gravy. Sometimes I would drop in on a little restaurant operated by a family of Jewish refugees from Austria and listen over a pastrami sandwich and dill pickle spears to their account of escape through Siberia and Manchuria. I spent much time reading American magazines and cheap copies of American books pirated by local printers. That was a mistake. I should have been studying Japanese; I had learned to speak it reasonably well but could not read or write it.

One day, the Municipal Council, Shanghai's governing body, made up of appointed representatives of the United States, Great Britain, France, and Japan, held an open-air meeting in a park in the Hongkew Japanese sector. I was standing at the back of the crowd when I saw an elderly Japanese, whom I identified as a well-known community leader, walk up on the platform where the councilmen sat. No one paid any attention to him; presumably he was going to consult with the Japanese representative. He moved deliberately behind the chairman, a Briton. As I watched, the Japanese pulled a small-caliber pistol from his coat pocket and fired two shots into the chairman's back. The assailant was quickly subdued, and the Brit, who was not badly injured, was hurried off to the hospital. There was no trial. The Japanese was spirited back to his country, and no more was said.

Some weeks earlier, the pro-Japanese mayor of Shanghai, an elderly Chinese who no doubt had been bought off, was hacked to death with a kitchen cleaver in the middle of the night as he slept. A member of his household whom I had come to know telephoned me with the news. I relayed the information to my friend Ken Murayama of Domei, and he filed a story to Tokyo before anyone else knew about it. Exciting? Yes. But I knew it was time for me to go home to the States.

The only air service across the Pacific at the time was via Pan American Clippers that island-hopped between San Francisco and Manila. Compared to the cost of ocean travel, airfare was prohibitively expensive. I should have booked passage directly from Shanghai to San Francisco on an American ship, but I wanted to see what was happening in Japan first. So I made reservations on the same vessel that had carried Alice from Yokohama to Seattle, packed my belongings, and in late July flew one of Japan's new commercial airliners to Tokyo.

My timing couldn't have been worse. As I was preparing to leave Shanghai, the United States froze all Japanese credits in an economic clampdown intended to force Tokyo to pull its troops out of China. That resulted in an immediate suspension of commercial relations between the two countries. Angered by Japanese defiance, Washington had taken this calculated risk. Unless Japan backed down and agreed to pull out of China—a totally unlikely response—the next step had to be war.

My flight to Tokyo was scheduled to stop at Fukuoka on Kyushu, the southernmost island in the Japanese archipelago. There, bad weather forced cancellation of the Tokyo leg. I hurried to the railroad station, bought a ticket, sat down to wait, and soon dozed off. Suddenly I heard an announcement that the train for Nagasaki was about to leave. Groggy with sleep, I thought I heard the announcer say the train was leaving for Shimonoseki, which was where I wanted to go. I raced to the train and leapt aboard as it was pulling out. A few minutes later, I realized I was headed in the wrong direction. A kindly conductor told me I could get off at the next station, catch a train back to Fukuoka, and be on my way. This is exactly what the hero in a spy movie would do to shake off a shadow, and I worried that my actions might arouse suspicion. On an earlier trip to Japan, I had been questioned by a glowering, unshaven plainclothesman who wanted to know who I was, where I was headed, and why. If he or one of his colleagues had been watching me on this trip, I might have wound up in a Japanese pokey.

In Tokyo I learned that all shipping between Japan and the United States had been suspended. I found myself stranded, with nothing to do but sit around and wait. After nearly a month, living off the generosity of friends, I cabled Charlie Laval in Shanghai and asked him to book me on the first available American ship sailing for the United States. Then I flew back to Shanghai. Laval told me I was at the bottom of a 600-name waiting list and that with luck I might be able to leave in a month.

I finally got word that there was space on the President Cleveland, leaving the first week of October. On a bright, moonlit night, I watched the lights of Shanghai fade away as the Cleveland slipped down the Whangpoo toward its rendezvous with the Yangtze. Home was nearly 5,000 miles away, but I was on my way.

There were four men assigned to our two-bunk cabin. I was one of the two who slept on canvas cots. The ship was jammed with business-men, missionaries and their families, a few tourists, and American ser-vicemen who had completed assignments in the Philippines, all anxious to get home. A few days out of Shanghai, I developed flu-like symptoms. The ship's doctor said I did indeed have the flu, with perhaps a touch of jaundice. There was no room in the infirmary, so I had to remain in my cabin, alternately sweating and shaking with chills. I don't know who was more uncomfortable—me or my cabinmates.

On a windy, late October day, the President Cleveland eased under the Golden Gate Bridge and docked in San Francisco. The Filipino cabin steward, understanding my plight, refused the few dollars I offered as a tip. My legs were still unsteady. I found a cheap hotel room, slept around the clock, and took a slow, slow train for Portland. Alice, with a big, bright-eyed boy named Mike in her arms, was waiting for me on the platform.

The attack on Pearl Harbor was less than a month and a half away.

Chapter Two

From the Fire Into the Frying Pan

On a bright, sunny Sunday morning, unusual for Seattle in December, I was raking leaves in the yard of my father's home when Alice appeared at the back door.

"Jack Maki's on the phone," she said.

Maki was an old friend. He had studied in Tokyo and had come home to teach Japanese literature at the University of Washington.

"Have you been listening to the radio?" he asked.

I hadn't; I'd been outside working.

"Well," Jack said calmly, "they've bombed Pearl Harbor."

The date was December 7, 1941. The news was unbelievable, yet I knew immediately what Jack was talking about. But it took a while for it to sink in that the Japanese had sailed undetected—how was that possible?—across thousands of miles of ocean and dared to launch a savage attack against the United States while their diplomats in Washington talked peace.

"Jesus Christ," I muttered. It was both a curse and a prayer. "What's going to happen now?" I asked Jack.

"Nothing very good for anybody," he said. "It's really hit the fan."

I was not surprised that the war the jingoists on both sides of the Pacific had been predicting for decades had come at last. For months, if not years, the two nations had been on a collision course, and the question was less what would happen than when it would happen. My experience in Shanghai made it clear that only at the risk of revolution could Japan pull out of China. And the United States could not afford to let the Japanese remain. Such an impasse could result only in violent collision. There was no doubt in my mind that Japan would be crushed in time by superior American manpower, firepower, and economic power, but both sides were capable of inflicting enormous suffering before the war ended.

My immediate concern was about what lay ahead for Japanese Americans like my wife and me, and more worrisome, what would happen to Japanese nationals like my parents. I had faith in civics texts that swore to the sanctity of the rights of citizenship (well, perhaps it is more accurate to say I made myself believe in them), but if the Japanese could sail halfway across the Pacific and sink our battleships, anything could happen. My greatest concern was for my parents, who had lived most of their adult lives in the United States and remained noncitizens only because the law denied them, like all Asians, the right of naturalization. I knew how cruelly German Americans had been treated in World War I, even though they were of the same racial stock as the overwhelming majority of Americans. This time, as the propaganda mills geared up to fan patriotic frenzy, and in view of the historic prejudice against Japanese immigrants living on the West Coast, I feared the war in the Pacific would quickly turn into a race war. Overnight, people like us would no longer be seen as Americans, but as "dirty, sneaky, slant-eyed, yellow-bellied Japs" and worse.

I could not remember seeing my parents more depressed than on that day. Japan was still their cultural and sentimental homeland, but America was where they had chosen to live. And America was the country of my birth. Now the two nations were at war; Japanese were killing Americans, and Americans were killing Japanese. Where did my parents' loyalties lie? Although they were Japanese, they would do nothing to hurt their adopted country. They were grieved and confused. An elderly Japanese gentleman summed up the conundrum: "If your mother and your father were fighting, who would you want to win? I want only to have them stop."

Jimmie Sakamoto, publisher of the Japanese American *Courier,* where I had worked while attending college, was old enough to remember the hostility toward German Americans in World War I. On the day after the attack, he summoned some of his friends, mainly leaders of the local Japanese American Citizens League (JACL), a patriotic civic organization with chapters in every large Japanese-American community, to a meeting. I was among those present. Sakamoto warned of difficult times ahead. He noted that the leaders of Seattle's Japanese American community, virtually all middle-aged or elderly aliens, had been rounded up by the FBI as possible security risks, leaving the others leaderless and confused.

Sakamoto proposed forming an Emergency Defense Council to serve as a liaison between the community and government officials, providing a two-way channel of communication. The council would also combat adverse public reaction and help Japanese American families in every way possible. Currently unemployed, I was named executive secretary.

The community—there were approximately 7,000 Japanese and Japanese Americans in the Seattle area—was in quiet, frightened turmoil and there was much to be done. Sakamoto had not exaggerated the problem. Within hours after the attack on Pearl Harbor, several hundred Issei—the foreign-born first generation of Japanese Americans— mostly community elders, had been arrested by the Federal Bureau of Investigation as potential security risks. Businesses were padlocked, bank accounts frozen. Insurance policies were canceled. Dozens of families had no cash to buy food or pay the rent. Some Issei employed outside the community—even cooks, clerks, and janitors—lost their jobs for no reason other than that they were Japanese. Fortunately, there had been no violence.

A few days after war's outbreak, Sakamoto invited Seattle mayor Earl Millikin to a community rally, which he hoped would assure the public of the loyalty of Japanese Americans, while at the same time easing the Japanese American community's anxieties. A crowd of 1,500 gathered at the newly built Buddhist temple, overflowing the main hall into the gymnasium and out into the street. Addressing the audience as "my fellow Americans," Millikin gave a rousing speech praising the loyalty of Japanese Americans and assuring them they had nothing to fear while he was mayor.

A few weeks later, he would tell a congressional committee that it was dangerous to trust Japanese Americans. Seattle, he said, was on the lookout for sabotage, and its mounted police corps was ready to escort the "Japs" over the Cascade Mountains into eastern Washington in case of emergency. So much for the integrity of our political friends.

Even Seattle PTA mothers succumbed to fear. Their leaders demanded the school board fire the twenty-seven Nisei girls employed as secretaries in principals' offices. Why? Because they might fail to relay air-raid warnings if an alarm were telephoned in to the schools. When the school board dithered, the girls resigned en masse to avoid controversy. A local newspaper, rather than chiding the school board for failing to stand by its employees, praised the girls for a "graceful act" that averted problems. Meanwhile, unknown to us, the army was preparing to kick us out of the West Coast. Old-time anti-Japanese organizations were pressuring the politicians, the politicians were pressuring the War Department, and the army, caught napping at Pearl Harbor, was frantically seeking ways to avoid phantom problems with "Japs" on the mainland.

The army's line of reasoning is revealed in the following excerpt of a recommendation, dated February 14, 1942, from Lieutenant General John L. DeWitt, chief of the Western Defense Command, to Secretary of War Henry Stimson:

> The Japanese race is an enemy race and while many second and third generation of Japanese born on United States soil, possessed of United States citizenship, have become "Americanized," the racial strains are undiluted. That Japan is allied with Germany and Italy in this struggle is no ground for assuming that any Japanese, barred from assimilation by convention as he is, though born and raised in the United States, will not turn against this nation when the final test of loyalty comes. It therefore follows that along the vital Pacific Coast over 112,000 potential enemies, of Japanese extraction, are at large today. There are indications that these are organized and ready for concerted action at a favorable opportunity. The very fact that no sabotage has taken place to date is a disturbing and confirming indication that such action will be taken.

Under the general's logic, the fact that there had been no disloyal acts was proof there would be treachery in the future and that it was only prudent to crack down on an entire racial segment of the population before anything happened. There were many who endorsed this point of view, although they were intelligent enough to have known better. Among the more ardent of General DeWitt's supporters were California attorney general Earl Warren, who would become chief justice of the U.S. Supreme Court, and Walter Lippmann, the eminent newspaper columnist credited in that era with Olympian wisdom.

On February 19, 1942, two months and eleven days after declaration of war—and with still no sign of the sabotage that Dewitt anticipated—President Franklin D. Roosevelt signed Executive Order 9066 in response to the general's fears. It authorized the army to designate areas from which "any or all persons" could be excluded. The broad significance of this presidential directive escaped almost everyone's notice until the army designated not just strategically important ports, airfields, factories, and power plants as forbidden zones, but the entire state of California, all of Alaska, half of Washington and Oregon, and a portion of Arizona. And the target of this exclusion order was everyone who was at least one-sixteenth Japanese. (Actually, the Japanese had not been in the United States long enough to produce offspring who were less than one half Japanese, and even these were rare because of anti-miscegenation laws.) The U.S. government was making this a race war. The fact that we also were also at war with Germany and Italy didn't appear to matter. Nor did it seem to concern Roosevelt that he was arbitrarily suspending the Bill of Rights—which guarantees citizens the protections of due process—for an entire American racial minority.

Evacuation orders, posted on walls and utility poles, were addressed to "all persons of Japanese ancestry." The army sidestepped the matter of citizens' Constitutional rights by specifying that the orders applied to both aliens and non-aliens. What is an non-alien? The irony of this demeaning euphemism did not escape those of us who were native-born American citizens of Japanese stock.

The situation was further confused by Congressman John H. Tolan, who announced that his committee would hold hearings to determine whether any special action against Japanese Americans was necessary. The first of the Tolan Committee hearings was set for San Francisco on February 21, two days after Roosevelt signed E.O. 9066 as a "military necessity." If this were indeed so critical a national defense matter, what purpose would be served by inviting members of the public to testify before a congressional committee after the ouster order had already been signed?

We were utterly naive about the hearings. We assumed they were an effort to ascertain facts about Japanese Americans and that we citizens were being given an opportunity to explain who we were, where our loyalties lay, and what we believed. The hearings turned out to be a public forum for "Jap"-haters to vent their spleen, with few bothering to distinguish between the Japanese enemy and Americans who happened to have Japanese forebears.

In Seattle, the strategy we adopted was to point out that Japanese Americans were loyal citizens and upstanding, productive members of the community who posed no security risk. We also intended to explain that we were important enough to the local economy that removing us would be damaging to the war effort. In retrospect, it was a mistake to focus on the economic implications rather than point out the violence being done to the Constitution. The legal argument undoubtedly would have carried little weight under the circumstances, but it certainly stood on higher moral ground.

Members of the Emergency Defense Council hurriedly gathered figures regarding, among other things, the number of grocery stores, cleaning shops, inexpensive restaurants, and rooming houses operated by Japanese Americans in Seattle, and how much lettuce, peas, celery, cabbage, and other fresh vegetables were grown by Japanese American farmers in western Washington. Working throughout the night before the hearing, I wrote a report intended to persuade the Tolan Committee that we were good, patriotic, well-integrated Americans determined to make an important contribution to winning the war, and that to remove us was unnecessary, unfair, and disruptive to the war effort. Under the circumstances, it was an irrelevant argument in a forum where it was largely assumed that race determined loyalty—or lack thereof.

One of the charges leveled against us was that we had failed to turn in spies in our midst. Implying a racial conspiracy, Colonel Karl R. Bendetsen, who supervised the entire Evacuation program, justified the army's actions in a speech before the prestigious Commonwealth Club in San Francisco with these words: "Contrary to other national or racial groups, the behavior of Japanese has been such that in not one single instance has any Japanese reported disloyalty on the part of another specific individual of the same race . . . a most ominous thing."

But if there were no instances of disloyalty, how could they be reported? Ironically, Japanese American activists of a later generation would charge that JACL leaders betrayed the community by failing to oppose the Evacuation and sought to curry the government's favor by turning in the names of suspected spies and saboteurs.

The Tolan Committee was not impressed by our plea. The army and its allies argued that the very fact of our concentration in certain industries—for example, farming—posed a danger. More to the point, the hearings were a sham. Even as the Tolan Committee held hearings in San Francisco, Portland, Seattle, Los Angeles, and other points, the army, with Roosevelt's blessing, was preparing to move us into concentration camps, allowing us to take only what we could carry.

The enormity of E.O. 9066 failed to sink in at first. Japanese Americans were inclined to say that if this was what our government, in its wisdom, was asking of us, if this was what it would take to win the war, then we had a patriotic duty to cooperate. Years later, sociologist Harry Kitano, who spent some of his high school years in a detention camp, would suggest, with some hyperbole, that we Japanese Americans were so foolishly obedient, so unquestioning in our desire to demonstrate our loyalty, that if the U.S. Army had ordered us to march to our deaths in gas ovens, we would have done so without protest.

The FBI, which had rounded up and imprisoned alien leaders at war's outbreak, was not prepared to assume that every citizen was loyal. At least three Japanese Americans in Seattle were summoned before a federal grand jury. Two were indicted. Under other circumstances, the charges would have been ridiculous. Thomas Masuda, a prominent Nisei attorney, was accused of photographing an Armistice Day parade with a home movie camera. How many of the tens of thousands who viewed the parade also took pictures? Kenji Ito, another attorney, was charged with having made a speech about Japan's China policy, which allegedly made him an unregistered foreign agent. Both were tried and acquitted.

I was the third to face the grand jury. The U.S. attorney asked whether I had worked for the Japanese consulate before the war. I had, for about a year in 1937 and 1938. He wanted to know what I did. I said

I worked as a secretary, writing letters in English for the consul. He asked if I had ever written a letter to the newspaper in Bremerton, where there was a naval base. When I said I couldn't remember, he produced a copy of a letter on a consulate letterhead with my signature on it. I said the signature was mine, so presumably I had written it. The letter was addressed to the newspaper's circulation department and asked for a copy of a back issue that carried a news item about warships arriving at the base. The grand jury found that writing such a letter was not an indictable offense.

However, on February 25, any doubt that the government meant business vanished when the army gave Japanese American families on Terminal Island, a fishing community near San Pedro, California, forty-eight hours to evacuate their homes. No arrangements were made for them; they were simply told to get out, leaving them unable to dispose of expensive boats and nets, homes, furnishings, and other personal possessions. Most of them found shelter in Los Angeles churches or moved in with friends. A month later, the Evacuation moved closer to home when the entire Japanese American population of Bainbridge Island, which lay just across Puget Sound from Seattle, was placed on a ferry boat and then aboard a train and sent into exile. The offense committed by these 258 people in fifty-four family units was that they had chosen to farm on a large island that lay athwart the main channel to Bremerton. Their destination was a camp called Manzanar near California's Death Valley, the only detention facility ready to accept them.

The army's strategy was to establish several dozen "assembly centers," primarily at fairgrounds and racetracks, where basic facilities such as electric power, water, and sewage lines were available. As soon as these sites were readied for occupancy, which meant little more than erecting a barbed wire fence around the grounds and building row upon row of crude sheds to house people, "exclusion areas" were blocked out in nearby locales and a timetable was set up for mass movement into the camps.

Despite the army's apparent logistical thoroughness, very little thought had been given to other problems likely to arise in the detention centers. After all, men, women, and children were involved—people secure in their homes one day who would become frightened, confused, resentful prisoners the next. At the suggestion of army officers responsible for evacuating the Seattle area, the Emergency Defense Council changed its focus to help with administration of the camp where the Seattle community was to be sent. Jimmie Sakamoto would continue to act as leader, and I would serve as his adjutant.

Employees of the Wartime Civil Control Authority, a hastily created federal agency, would run the camps; Sakamoto's Evacuation Administration Headquarters would serve as a buffer between jail keepers and inmates and try to address human needs. Key roles in headquarters went to Sakamoto's associates in the Japanese American Citizens League because he knew them. As a result, certain individuals who were not close to Sakamoto felt slighted, and this later led to friction.

One day, before the relocation, Sakamoto and I and several other members of the council were asked as a matter of courtesy to review Seattle evacuation plans the police department had drawn up for the army. There was a map on the wall with black lines outlining the areas, each with approximately the same population, to be evacuated during each phase. One zone covered what was known as the Western Avenue district, which was near the waterfront. Police figures showed that 500 to 600 Japanese Americans lived in the zone. I sensed something strange, but for a moment I couldn't put my finger on it. Then it came to me. "Wait a minute," I said. "What you have blocked out is the wholesale produce district. Nobody lives there. Lots of Japanese Americans come to work there early in the morning from homes in all parts of town. By the middle of the afternoon, they're through for the day, and there's nobody in the district except office workers." Red-faced, the police took the map away for revision.

The prospect of being locked up in camps was uninviting under any circumstances. Before exclusion orders were posted, a few families with friends in the nation's interior packed bare necessities into their cars and headed inland, which they were permitted to do. The word that came back was discouraging. Some families encountered roadblocks and were permitted to drive through towns only if they promised not to stop. Denied restaurant service, many picked up bologna and bread for sandwiches at grocery stores and slept in their cars. Before long, with the threat of violence growing, the army halted all "voluntary evacuation."

Before the freeze, my brother Bob decided to take care of a personal matter that some other Japanese Americans faced. His fiancee,

Yoshi Yoshizawa, lived with her parents in the outskirts of Portland, Oregon. Rather than accept the uncertainties of separation, Bob and Yoshi decided to marry so they could be interned at the same camp. The army, as if it didn't have more critical matters to attend to, issued her a pass enabling her to come to Seattle. She and Bob were married in a quiet church service, and they moved into my father's house with the rest of us. Their future was as uncertain as mine. Bob had a liberal arts degree from Whitman College in eastern Washington, where he had made Phi Beta Kappa, but had been working as a salesman in a furniture store. Now, with evacuation pending, even that job would soon be gone. But like so many other young couples of the time, they managed. After the war, Bob enjoyed a long career as a newspaperman, public relations counselor, and college professor. He and Yoshi celebrated their golden wedding anniversary in 1992 in Florida, where they retired.

The state fairgrounds at Puyallup, which I had visited occasionally in happier times, was the assembly center for Seattle evacuees. Some bureaucrat with a misguided sense of humor named it Camp Harmony. The first contingent entered the grounds on April 28, 1942, and several hundred others were processed through the gates every few days until it reached capacity—approximately 7,400 men, women, and children.

On "E-day" for each phase, residents of specified Seattle areas assembled with their suitcases in a sparsely built-up area just south of Chinatown. Soldiers with bayonet-tipped rifles, standing guard near a fleet of Greyhound buses, discouraged sight-seers. Each day I would go to the assembly area to help load luggage, console friends, and try to revive spirits.

E-day for our family arrived on May 15. The previous night, we had slept on the floor of our empty house. My father's car and furniture had been sold for a fraction of their value; treasured mementos, dishes, and kitchen utensils had been stored with friends and neighbors. We did not know when we would come back, if ever.

Puyallup is perhaps an hour's drive from Seattle. The bus ride was anything but fun. The caravan, escorted by military vehicles, made its way into the fairgrounds through a gate in a high barbed wire fence. In an instant we were transformed from free American citizens to prisoners in our own country.

Alice, Mike, and I were assigned a dark cubicle in a low wooden structure perhaps 150 feet long that resembled nothing more than a shed on a chicken ranch. The cubicles were separated from each other by partitions that did not reach the ceiling. We soon discovered that a baby wailing at one end of the structure could be heard at the other. Each unit had a window in the back wall and was furnished with steel cots and a single electric drop cord, nothing more. We were fortunate to get mattresses; some of the others were given mattress ticking and told to fill them with straw. Later, we found old orange crates and packing boxes to use as tables and chairs.

The toilet, washbasins, and showers were several hundred feet away under the fairground grandstand. There were only a few drinking fountains scattered around the area. Unless we had brought along a thermos bottle or teakettle for water storage, we walked to the grandstand to get a drink. Inside the fence, we were all equals, regardless of education, social status, religion, occupation, or wealth, made one by our common Japanese heritage.

Everyone was fed cafeteria-style in mess halls. Our first evening meal consisted of a boiled potato and canned Vienna sausage and bread and margarine. The food improved somewhat as restaurant chefs among the evacuees were allowed to take over.

After the shakedown period, boredom was the greatest enemy. Members of the Evacuee Administration Headquarters (the name had been modified to reflect the fact that the Evacuation had been completed and we were now evacuees, with new needs) took on new volunteer duties as activities leaders, mediators between unhappy internees and the civilian camp administrators, and bearers of complaints about bad food, plugged drains, the dust that rose when the grounds weren't watered down, and the endless variety of other complaints to J. J. McGovern, a federal civil service employee who had been given the job of camp director.

On the other side of the barbed wire, life went on as usual in the town of Puyallup. Traffic drove by, radio music and the smell of cooking drifted into the camp from homes across the street. Occasionally youngsters came by to "look at the Japs" as though we were animals in a zoo. We were allowed to receive and send out mail, buy newspapers, visit with each other, and take part in the arts and other classes we organized. We were even allowed to meet visitors on Sunday in a special fenced-in area. But we did not have what we wanted most: freedom.

Two events at the camp remain vivid even after half a century. On the morning of June 12, 1942, we awoke to find soldiers, armed with machine guns and in field uniform, staring down at us from atop the grandstand roof. Until then, the guards had been fairly unobtrusive. What had happened? We learned soon enough that Japanese naval planes had dropped a few bombs on Dutch Harbor in the far western Aleutians off Alaska, and enemy troops had landed on several nearby islands. If our jail keepers had anticipated a celebration or uprising in the camp, they were disappointed.

The other event was more personal. My son Mike had been fretful and was running a fever. Camp doctors said he had the mumps and needed to be isolated. Because he wasn't sick enough to be hospitalized outside the camp and the camp infirmary had no isolation ward, one had to be improvised. The doctors' solution was to place two cots in a cavernous, drafty, unoccupied exhibition barn in one corner of the fairgrounds and move Alice and Mike into it. Alice provided the only nursing care. They were allowed no visitors, but I was permitted to bring them meals from the camp kitchen.

I went to see McGovern and demanded better treatment for my family. Frozen-faced, he said he was sympathetic. But he did nothing. I sensed I had been marked as too outspoken, a potential troublemaker.

When we were ordered out of our homes, there had been no indication as to when we would be allowed to return. As spring changed to summer, it became increasingly evident that the government had no plans to release us. By midsummer, the tide of war had changed. The Battle of Midway crippled the Japanese fleet. The invasion of the Aleutians was short-lived. All along the Pacific front, Japanese forces were retreating rather than attacking, and any further threat against the U.S. mainland seemed unlikely, even to armchair strategists. Yet there was no indication that we would regain our freedom anytime soon. Temporary removal from potentially strategic areas in the face of a supposed military threat had turned into indefinite imprisonment.

There was time now to recall high school civics lessons and to ask why we continued to be locked up. Some examined the Constitution in books they had brought with them. What they found was profoundly disturbing. There could be no doubt that our Constitutional guarantees had been violated. And the American public, with the exception of a few human rights advocates, had watched the rape without protest—and in many cases, with a certain satisfaction.

The Fifth Amendment specifies that "no persons shall be held to answer for a capital, or otherwise infamous crime, unless on a presentment or indictment of a Grand Jury . . . nor be deprived of life, liberty, or property without due process of law." Had there been due process of law in our imprisonment?

The Sixth Amendment states that "in all criminal prosecutions, the accused shall enjoy the right to a speedy and public trial . . . and to be informed of the nature and cause of the accusation; to be confronted with the witnesses against him." There had been no trial prior to our detention and no accusation of wrongdoing—other than being members of a particular race.

The Fourteenth Amendment provides that no state "shall deprive any person of life, liberty, or property, without due process of law, nor deny to any person within its jurisdiction the equal protection of the laws."

Phrases like "due process," "speedy and public trial," and "equal protection of the laws," hallowed in the history of the United States, were meaningless at Camp Harmony and the other camps where Japanese Americans languished.

In a sense, it might be said that by submitting to the army's evacuation orders—was there an alternative?—we had accepted suspension of our civil rights. But this was not entirely true. Four Japanese Americans sought justice in legal challenges that went all the way to the Supreme Court. Two of the plaintiffs were Minoru Yasui, a Portland attorney, and Gordon Hirabayashi, a Seattle college student.

Yasui was offended by government orders that distinguished between citizens on the grounds of ancestry. He protested the curfew orders, applicable only to persons of Japanese origins, that preceded the Evacuation. Yasui notified federal authorities of his intention to test the order by violating the curfew, was arrested, found guilty, and spent nine months in solitary confinement before he was sent to the Minidoka relocation camp in Idaho.

Hirabayashi, a devout Quaker, resisted the Evacuation as a matter of conscience. He could not reconcile God's will, expressed in the Bill of Rights and the Constitution, with the order discriminating against Japanese Americans. Like Yasui, he asked to be arrested and be heard in court. There he was found guilty of violating Evacuation orders and sentenced to serve in a road camp.

Fred Korematsu, a California welder, resisted the Evacuation for altogether different reasons. He wanted to stay out of the camps and marry his girlfriend, who was not subject to Evacuation orders (she soon rejected him). He underwent plastic surgery to change his appearance and went into hiding. He was carrying a fake draft card, denied he was a Japanese American, and gave a false name when he was apprehended in a forbidden zone after several weeks of dodging the authorities.

The fourth litigant was Mitsuye Endo, a clerk in the California state civil service system who was fired after Pearl Harbor because of her ancestry. She was evacuated along with other Japanese Americans to the Tanforan racetrack. Her court challenge was based on the writ of habeus corpus; her attorney argued that under the law, she was entitled to be charged without delay, given a trial, and freed if the charges could not be proved. As it was, the only reason for her detention was that she was of Japanese descent, and even assuming this was a crime, she was never given her day in court.

Because Constitutional issues were involved, all four cases eventually came before the Supreme Court. The first of the decisions was returned in December 1944, three years and eleven days after Pearl Harbor. Only Mitsuye Endo's habeus corpus plea led to freedom. The others were convicted of violating federal laws.

Many years later, there was a startling development. While researching the four Japanese American cases, Professor Peter Irons, a legal historian at the University of California, San Diego, uncovered evidence that government attorneys had deliberately concealed or distorted evidence favorable to the defendants in their appearances before the Supreme Court. In a book entitled *Justice at War* (Oxford University Press, 1983), Irons charged the government with "a legal scandal without precedent in the history of American law." "Never before," he wrote, "has evidence emerged that shows a deliberate campaign to present tainted records to the Supreme Court."

Teams of volunteer Sansei attorneys for Yasui, Hirabayashi, and Korematsu filed new appeals under an obscure legal measure—*writ of habeus corpus corum nobis*—which in practice means that a review is being sought because something new has been discovered to affect an earlier verdict.

Dale Minami, lead attorney for Korematsu's appeal, wrote that the evidence revealed "a government determined to win the three cases without regard to legal ethics or the rights of the defendants."

In San Francisco, Judge Marilyn Hall Patel annulled Korematsu's conviction. Subsequently, government attorneys, in candid admission of miscarriage of justice, asked federal courts to reverse the convictions of Yasui and Hirabayashi.

Early in 1998, Korematsu received the Presidential Medal of Freedom, the nation's most prestigious award for service to the country, in recognition of his fight for justice. Some Japanese Americans asked why Korematsu alone was honored while his co-litigants, Yasui and Hirabayashi, who had been moved by more impressive motives, were ignored. In view of President Clinton's widely publicized extracurricular proclivities, perhaps we should not have been surprised.

Late in the spring of 1942, the Japanese American Citizens League shifted its national headquarters from the prohibited San Francisco area to Salt Lake City, which was in the "free" zone. It also converted its sporadically published newspaper, the *Pacific Citizen,* into a weekly that would serve as a communication link among dispersed Japanese Americans. Larry Tajiri, a crackerjack journalist who lost his job in New York when the war broke out, moved to Salt Lake City to take over as editor. The first issue under Tajiri's direction was published on June 4, 1942. Copies reached the Puyallup camp a few days later. I saw the value of the paper and wanted to be a part of it. I wrote to Tajiri and asked whether he would entertain contributions. Tajiri responded with an invitation to write a comment column on a regular basis.

The weekly column that was born has appeared, with only a few interruptions, for more than a half century. I titled it "From the Frying Pan," alluding to my leap from the fierce fire of war in Shanghai into the uncomfortable frying pan of the Evacuation. Tajiri gave me complete freedom. Some of my columns were angry. Some were philosophical or whimsical but invariably upbeat. Some were wry commentaries on life.

Some had to do with humorous problems of living "on the outside," of raising children, of being yellow-skinned in a nation of white-skinned people. Over the years, the column picked up a following, and in 1978, McGraw-Hill published the best of my efforts in a book titled *Thirty-five Years in the Frying Pan*. But I am getting ahead of the story.

In early August 1942, it was announced that everyone would soon be moved from the Puyallup camp to a new, semipermanent facility being built on the sagebrush flats near Twin Falls, Idaho, where the Minidoka irrigation project provided water for farming. This news killed all hope that the government would permit us to go home in the foreseeable future. However, a larger site would be a vast improvement over the cramped, primitive facilities at the Puyallup fairgrounds. An advance crew of volunteers, including my brother and his bride, left Puyallup on August 12 to prepare for the mass movement.

Two days later, I was summoned to McGovern's office at 2 P.M.. Dispensing with the preliminaries, he told me right off that I would not be going to Minidoka. My wife and son and I were being sent to another camp in Heart Mountain, Wyoming. At 5 P.M., we were to report with our belongings at the main gate, where a government escort would take us to the railroad station for the trip to Wyoming.

I asked why I was being separated from my friends.

"I don't know," McGovern said with a shrug. "I have my orders."

I believed then that he was not telling the truth, and I have found no reason to change my mind. Documents from that era are scarce, but I have discovered some interesting material pried from federal archives through the Freedom of Information Act. In an August 3, 1942, memorandum stamped "Confidential," Lieutenant Colonel A. K. Stebbins at Western Defense Command Headquarters in Fort Lewis, Washington, wrote to the assistant chief of staff G–2 at Fourth Army Headquarters at the Presidio in San Francisco. In the memo, he refers to a July 27, 1942, letter from the Seattle branch of the G-2 section discussing the activities of Tom Masuda, Kenji Ito, and William Hosokawa. The July 27 letter has not been found, but the final paragraph of the August 3 memo says:

> It is recommended that action be taken through the Wartime
> Civil Control Administration to arrange the transfer of Masuda,
> Ito and Hosokawa to a different relocation center than that to

which the personnel from Puyallup are taken, and to send each of them to a separate relocation center. It is believed that such action would greatly reduce the possibility of internal dissatisfaction at the Minnedoka [*sic*] Center, as well as placing Masuda, Ito, and Hosokawa where they cannot combine their efforts.

In another army memorandum dated August 7, the War Relocation Authority, which ran the permanent camps, was instructed to transfer Ito, Masuda, Hosokawa, and one Roy Suyetani, along with their families, to different War Relocation Projects "as soon as possible in view of the fact these evacuees as a group are disturbing factions in the assembly center. The activities of each prior to December, 1941, were unsatisfactory from a counter-intelligence standpoint. In view of same, it is also unsatisfactory for all to be in the same assembly center or relocation project."

On August 12, Suyetani, his wife, and two children were sent off to the Gila River WRA camp in Arizona. Kenji Ito, his wife, and child were sent to Tule Lake camp in California. Tom Masuda, his wife Kikuye, and Fuku Otoni (relationship unknown) were sent to the Colorado River camp in Arizona. And my wife, son, and I were sent to Heart Mountain, Wyoming.

Just two days later, on August 14, the Seattle office of G–2 sent another "Confidential" message to Fourth Army Headquarters. It said, in part, that "the removal of Hosokawa, Ito, Suyetani and Masuda to different relocation centers has had a very good effect at the Camp. Not only has it removed these four subversive characters to separate locations, but it has indicated to the persons remaining at the Camp that disciplinary action may be the result of un-American agitation." The memo went on to recommend the banishment of four other individuals, among them my father, Setsugo Hosokawa, who was considered subversive because "S. Hosokawa is the father of William Hosokawa and was largely instrumental in encouraging Thomas Masuda to be active in the Japanese Association, and further was associated with Masuda in the Japanese Prefectural Club."

The Japanese Association functioned like a chamber of commerce and looked after the welfare of Japanese nationals in the community. The Prefectural Club was a social organization composed of immigrants who had come from the same Japanese prefecture, or state. Unknown to the army, at the time the memorandum was written, my father was no longer at Camp Harmony. He and my mother had been sent from Puyallup to Minidoka in the course of a routine transfer. For some reason, the army then lost interest in him. It is strange that he was considered too dangerous and disruptive to be kept at Puyallup but not dangerous among the same people at Minidoka.

My father remained in Minidoka until the camp was closed at the end of the war. He returned to Seattle and died in 1952, unaware that preserved in the federal archives were documents that branded him as subversive for reasons that he would not have understood. He had lived by choice in the United States for fifty-three years. The last time he visited Japan was several decades before war's outbreak. My mother died in 1947, less than three years after returning to Seattle; her chronic kidney and heart condition had not been improved by camp life.

The imprisonment of Alice's mother, Tora Miyake, was even more deplorable. After the death of her husband in 1936, she eked out a living giving piano lessons, teaching part-time at a Japanese-language school, and working as a printer at the family's little weekly newspaper. She was among the few women jailed by the FBI. She was shy and retiring, weighed barely 100 pounds, and rarely left her two-room apartment in a run-down downtown hotel except to go to work. It is difficult to imagine a less likely security risk. We thought at first that she had been mistaken for her late husband, whose name, Taro, sounded similar. As a newspaper editor prominent in the Portland community, he seemed the more likely "threat" to national security. Later, we learned that anyone who taught in Japanese-language schools was automatically on the FBI's pickup list.

Even as she was waiting to be sent to an alien detention camp in Texas, her son Kenneth Miyake quit college to enlist in the U.S. Army. He earned a Combat Infantryman Badge and a Purple Heart while serving with the Nisei 442nd Regimental Combat Team in Italy and France.

It was difficult for me to imagine that my mother-in-law was considered a security risk, and harder still to fathom why I, too, was considered subversive, a designation no less unpleasant now than back in 1942. An anonymously written document in the files of the Thirteenth Naval

District, marked "Confidential" until released by the authorities a few years ago, contains the following information:

> When it became certain that evacuation of the Japanese was inevitable, the local chapters of the Japanese American Citizens League seemingly cooperated wholeheartedly with the designated evacuation authorities. . . . With the knowledge and approval of the U.S. military authorities in charge of the evacuation, the Seattle Japanese American Citizens League prepared, along military lines, an organization known as the "Evacuation Administration Headquarters" that was to be in charge of the internal administration of the Puyallup Assembly Center under the Caucasian staff of the Wartime Civil Control Administration.
>
> At the Puyallup Assembly Center the "Evacuee Administration Headquarters" under the leadership of James Yoshinori Sakamoto succeeded in maintaining harmony and peace for a period of from six weeks to two months. Friction then broke out when a rival group led by Thomas Shinao Masuda and Kenji Ito, both Seattle Nisei attorneys, who had just succeeded in gaining acquittal in Federal Court on charges of being unregistered agents of the Japanese government, challenged the JACL group's authority. Sakamoto's supporters, in endeavoring to maintain their authority, adopted the stand that as loyal patriotic Americans the Nisei should make the best of the camp, which was to be a temporary inconvenience at most, and do all possible to cooperate with the U.S. government in every way. The opposition, led by Masuda and Ito, are supported by most of the Kibei group (American born but educated in Japan) and the most pro-Japan element among the alien body, argued that the internal camp administration was undemocratic and un-American because its officers were not duly elected by popular vote and that the JACL was a tool of the U.S. government agencies such as the Army, Navy, and Federal Bureau of Investigation, and had been remiss in its duty to its members and the Japanese community in general when it failed to fight the evacuation orders (at least as pertaining to the Nisei) in the courts.

To ascertain the view of the Japanese in the camp . . . the camp supervisor called for a vote of confidence in the Japanese American Citizens League and its administrative setup at Camp Harmony. All (adult) evacuees at the center were given the opportunity to vote. An overwhelming margin of nearly five to one in favor of retaining the Japanese American Citizens League internal administrative body results.

Failing to gain internal control of the center, Masuda and his group commenced to use all available means to bring discredit to the assembly centers, the Wartime Civil Control Authority administrator and all others having any part in the evacuation of the Japanese.

The election mentioned is very dim in my memory, and I have no idea whether the charges against Masuda and Ito had any substance. Nor do I understand how I became associated with them in the minds of the military. It is difficult to understand why anyone would want to stage what amounted to a coup d'etat in a situation where there was no self-government and those of us working to improve our situation were without authority.

One naval intelligence document identifies me as a supporter of the Masuda-Ito faction, which presumably turned against Sakamoto in some manner. Even if that were true, I don't see how that made me subversive. Prior to the war, I had known Masuda and Ito casually, the way I knew scores of other Japanese Americans in Seattle, but I had never consulted them professionally and can recall no substantive conversations with them. I had never met the other member of the so-called cabal, Roy Suyetani, and knew nothing about him.

But these were paranoid times, with a four-star general urging his country to view an entire racial minority as potential spies and saboteurs, and the findings of amateur sleuths being given great credence by an inexperienced and probably frightened military intelligence establishment. What is even more distressing is the permanence of false and unproven intelligence findings. Baseless allegations recorded a half century ago remain in the files long after the maligned are dead. Not long ago, it was reported that FBI archives record that the late Arthur Goldberg—former justice of the Supreme Court, ambassador to the

United Nations, and secretary of labor under President Kennedy—was suspected of Communist ties and targeted for possible detention as a national security risk prior to World War II. More recently, an FBI dossier on James Baker, secretary of state during the Bush administration, was among security files discovered under curious circumstances in the Clinton White House.

Even today I don't know whether to laugh or cry about my encounter with the national security apparatus—laugh because the documents show our intelligence service was so incredibly naive and misinformed that I wonder how we won the war, or cry because of the arrogant, heartless, and stupid way my country sought to preserve democracy.

Word of my impending departure from Puyallup spread quickly. A large throng gathered at the main gate to bid me and Alice and Mike goodbye. The crowd was largely silent, bewildered, giving only an occasional shout of encouragement. I stepped through the gate, and suddenly my eyes filled with tears. Even though my family and I were still under guard, for the first time in three months we were outside the barbed wire fence.

Chapter Three

The Comeback Years

The guard assigned to escort this "subversive" and his family to a locale where he could do no mischief was remarkably laid-back. There was no bulge under his jacket betraying a concealed pistol, no handcuffs dangling from his hip pocket. He sat in another part of the railroad coach and made himself completely unobtrusive. After dark, Alice and Mike were taken to a Pullman sleeper. I sat upright in the coach. Sleep eluded me as I tried to sort out everything that had happened and wondered about what lay ahead.

Early next morning, the train stopped in Spokane. It was as far east as I had been in the United States. The guard waved his permission when I said I wanted to pick up a newspaper and some candy bars. After all, he had my wife and child as hostages. No one in the station noticed me as I hurried to a newsstand. That evening, we left the train at Billings, Montana, and stayed overnight at an inexpensive hotel near the depot. In the morning, we boarded another train for the journey across the parched Montana plain to a sunburned junction called Deaver just across the Wyoming border.

A friendly young man with a New York accent introduced himself as Bill Friedman and took custody of us on behalf of the War Relocation Authority (WRA), which was responsible for running the semipermanent camps. On the short drive—perhaps twenty-five miles or so—to the Heart Mountain campsite, Friedman said he had been hired as city planner.

I could see he had either a huge opportunity or none at all. What was to become Heart Mountain Camp was a square mile bustling with intense activity. Hundreds of one-story army-type barracks sheathed in ugly black tar paper had been erected in precise blocks, and swarms of carpenters were building scores of others. Tractors and trucks rumbled about, tearing up the sagebrush that dotted the landscape and raising great clouds of alkali dust. Water and sewer pipes were being laid, power lines strung.

One of the carpenters was a teenager from nearby Lovell who, like so many other Wyoming youngsters, had quit his summer job to take a higher-paid position with a construction crew at the "Jap camp." His name was Cal Taggart, and he grew up to run a prosperous insurance business. Many years later, after he had served as mayor of Lovell and then as Wyoming state senator, I got to know him. He had developed an intense interest in the camp and the issues involved in its creation. We became good friends.

It was obvious as we approached the campsite that an enormous amount of work remained before what was to become Wyoming's third-largest city would be ready for the 10,000 West Coast exiles scheduled to be confined there. Some 200 of them, an advance party paving the way for others to follow, were already housed in Blocks 1 and 2. They were from the Pomona Assembly Center on the outskirts of Los Angeles. I didn't know any of them.

Mike, Alice, and I were assigned to Block 1, Barrack 19, Unit A. It consisted of one room, somewhat smaller than a double garage, with no ceiling or inside walls other than the sheetrock that separated it from the next room. It was an end room with three windows—front, back, and end. This was a dubious blessing. All the windows were loosely fitted, which made our "apartment" triply vulnerable to dust storms or winter blizzards. The room came furnished with a heavy layer of Wyoming dust, one drop-cord electrical outlet, three metal army cots, and a huge cylindrical cast-iron coal-burning space heater indispensable in an uninsulated room in an area where temperatures dropped as low as thirty degrees below zero. The mess hall and the bathroom, with stools lined up in an unpartitioned room, were about 200 feet away. Our next-door neighbors, in a room the same size as ours, were Los Angeles gardener Ray Hifumi, his semi-invalid wife, three adolescent daughters, and one teenage son.

Responsibility for the camps fell to WRA's director in Washington, D.C., Dillon S. Myer, a career civil servant with the Department of Agriculture who before the war had scarcely been aware that Japanese Americans existed. Of course, he had no experience running concentration camps—who in the American bureaucracy did?—but before long, we found he was blessed with courage and good instincts, which overcame many shortcomings. The various departments under his direction were responsible for feeding and housing the inmates, providing medical and police and fire protection, educating the children, setting up work projects and recreation programs, maintaining the account books, operating the water and sewage systems, and keeping the residents—they were not to be called prisoners—from becoming too dissatisfied with life in the ten camps. Myer would soon discover, however, that the most demanding part of his job was not running the camps but fending off the intemperate attacks of certain members of Congress, the press, and a variety of publicity-seeking superpatriots who complained that we were being pampered at government expense.

In each of the ten camps, the population would rocket from zero to as many as 20,000 within a few weeks. As a result, all of the camps were built hastily—in inhospitable and remote sections of federal land that no one wanted. In addition to Manzanar, California had a second camp in the bed of a former swamp called Tule Lake near the Oregon border. There were two camps in Arizona, two in Arkansas that were soon combined into a single facility in the Mississippi River bottoms, and one each in parched areas of Idaho, Utah, Colorado, and Wyoming. Military police—who could have been put to better use in combat—were stationed outside each camp, charged with manning the watchtowers to make sure that we didn't escape. Escape to where? In Wyoming, there was nothing but brush-covered hills and mountains as far as we could see.

The various operational departments in each camp were headed by federal civil servants and staffed by evacuees holding subordinate positions. It was soon discovered, however, that many of these Japanese Americans knew more about running the departments than their government supervisors. Those of us who served in this "professional" capacity were paid $19 a month, as compared to the $12 and $16 dollars paid unskilled workers.

On my first day in Heart Mountain, I met Vaughn "Bonnie" Mechau, head of the Reports (Information) Department. He would become my boss and friend. Bonnie was a jolly, somewhat overweight former news-paperman who had a fondness for beer and disdain for government red tape, a conviction that the Evacuation was wrong, and a commitment to make camp life as pleasant as possible for the inmates. Among them, he may have been the most popular staff member. One of his responsibili-ties was to set up a camp newspaper, and when he discovered my back-ground, he invited me to help found it.

Bonnie introduced me to the project director, Chris Rachford, a craggy-faced Forest Service veteran. After a reasonable amount of small talk, I asked if he knew why I had come to Heart Mountain under some-what clouded circumstances. He said he did not—the same response I had gotten from McGovern in Puyallup—but this time I believed it. I told him that if I had to remain at Heart Mountain indefinitely, I didn't want some mysterious stigma keeping me from a meaningful work as-signment. "Don't worry," he replied, "there'll be plenty of work around here for everybody."

Before long, trainloads of hot, weary, apprehensive evacuees be-gan arriving at Heart Mountain every few days. Some of the trains had made their way leisurely, with armed soldiers enforcing the order to keep shades drawn, from the Los Angeles area to northwestern Wyoming by way of El Paso, Texas, across endless plains shimmering in the heat. There was, of course, no air-conditioning. The people in the advance party checked them in, escorted them to one of the mo-notonously stark, dusty rooms that would be home for the foreseeable future, and showed them to the showers, where they could wash off the sweat and grime before picking up a sandwich and a cold drink at the mess hall.

Meanwhile, Bonnie and I were talking with Jack Richard, editor and general manager of the *Cody Enterprise,* a weekly newspaper pub-lished in the town of Cody a dozen miles southwest of the campsite. After some calculating, Richard said he could rustle up enough news-print for up to 6,000 copies of a weekly eight-page tabloid newspaper.

Because the *Enterprise* came out Thursdays, type for the camp paper would have to be set during the week and printed on the clunky old flatbed press on Friday night for Saturday delivery.

The next steps in creating a newspaper duplicated what I had done in Singapore. A staff had to be assembled and assignments made, headline type selected and style established, prototype issues put together to determine how the paper would look, a name chosen and a masthead created. Fortunately there were experienced journalists in the camp. I chose Haruo Imura, a veteran of Japanese American newspapers in San Francisco, as managing editor. Louise Suski, who had worked on the staff of the *Rafu Shimpo* in Los Angeles, became city editor. Michi Onuma of San Francisco took over as business manager. And a number of enthusiastic and talented younger men and women joined the staff as writers.

The most critical decision involved editorial policy. Bonnie and I agreed that the newspaper's primary function was to report news of interest and concern to the people it served, not unlike any small-town weekly, but different in significant ways. This meant reporting on activities and developments within Heart Mountain and on other news pertaining to Japanese Americans as a whole. Included would be news about WRA activities and directives, actions in Congress affecting Japanese Americans, and reports about happenings nationwide either hostile or favorable toward us.

Beyond reporting the news, the newspaper should have the right and obligation to comment on the news in its editorial page and be a vehicle for airing reader opinion. This was a tricky responsibility. After all, the newspaper existed at the will of WRA. Could such a newspaper criticize the agency that had given it life? If so, to what extent? Bonnie and I agreed the newspaper should not serve as a WRA mouthpiece, but neither should it snipe constantly at WRA.

Early on, we discovered WRA was just about the only friend we had in government. President Roosevelt and the army had imprisoned us. Some members of Congress were demanding that men and women in the camps be separated so we wouldn't breed like rabbits. Others were saying we should be deported, although it doesn't seem possible to deport native-born citizens. Virtually no voices were raised in Congress in our defense. WRA, on the other hand, impressed us that it had our interests at heart, that it was doing the best it could under unprecedented circumstances.

The staff agreed to name the paper the *Heart Mountain Sentinel* for several reasons: "Sentinel" is a good, traditional newspaper name; Heart Mountain stood, in fact, like a sentinel over the camp; and we saw the paper as a sentinel watching over the rights and interests of its readers. The first issue was published on October 24, 1942, and sold for $.03 per copy through the camp co-op canteens. The price was soon reduced to $.02; we did not have to make a profit, and payroll was not a problem, as every member of the staff was paid his or her pittance by WRA. The initial press run of 3,000 copies sold out quickly. We ordered another 1,500 copies, which also sold out. Before long, we were printing our allotment of 6,000 copies and selling out consistently. The post office reported thousands of copies were being mailed out each week to friends and former neighbors back home.

The *Sentinel* had a dual responsibility. It had to give voice to its readers' anger, supporting their demands for justice and providing articulate leadership, but it also had to be cautious about fueling the anger of citizens unjustly imprisoned. Achieving this middle ground was difficult, and the balance often precarious, as we discovered shortly after publication began.

The issue that tested the *Sentinel*'s mettle and WRA's commitment to free speech was the army's decision to surround the campsite with a three-strand barbed wire fence and watchtowers every few hundred feet. One of the first things the inmates had noticed and appreciated when they arrived in Heart Mountain was the absence of a fence. The high woven wire fences surrounding the assembly centers had been bitterly resented. As it turned out, the unfenced Heart Mountain camp was not evidence of the government's sensitivity or understanding; it simply hadn't gotten around to stringing the barbed wire, and now it was ready to get the job done.

A three-strand fence was sufficient to stop cattle but useless in confining anyone determined to slip out. Beyond the fence there was nothing but sagebrush desert for miles in any direction. The evacuees felt there was no need for such a fence. It was seen as merely another government device to humiliate us. And because we were told that we had been moved inland for our own protection, the fence was viewed as further evidence of the government's treachery.

The order to erect the fence created so much resentment that 3,000 signatures were collected on a petition to Myer requesting that it and the guard towers be removed forthwith. Under a headline that stretched across the top of page one, the *Sentinel* published a story about the protest, including the petition's text. An editorial acknowledged the tension in the camp and praised both residents and administrators for patience in addressing a difficult problem.

In retrospect, I think the *Sentinel* should have taken a more forthright editorial position. But at a time when we were still feeling our way, simply being allowed to publish the news seemed a triumph for press freedom. As it turned out, the *Sentinel*'s calm handling of an incendiary situation helped avoid a potentially ugly confrontation. WRA soon modified its policy so residents could leave the campsite during daylight hours if they wished to look for arrowheads or capture a rattlesnake.

Two weeks after the fence episode, the *Sentinel* published a strongly worded but quixotic guest editorial from the chairman of the Block Administrators Council demanding total removal of the fence and immediate restoration of the rights suspended by the Evacuation. Of course, nothing happened, but the fact that we published it made up somewhat for the weak editorial.

Readers were particularly encouraged when the *Sentinel* stood up aggressively against unfair attacks on Japanese Americans by politicians and superpatriots. Wyoming's Senator E. V. Robertson had been a particularly loud critic of what he called "coddling of the evacuees" at Heart Mountain. However, he had never visited the camp, although his ranch home was only a few miles away. We composed a telegram inviting the senator to visit Heart Mountain before posing as an expert, and Bonnie Mechau paid from his own pocket to send the message via Western Union. Then we reported what we had done in a front-page story. The senator did not respond and never did visit the camp, but our readers considered our stunt great fun.

The *Sentinel* also took on the mighty *Denver Post,* which in those days had a reputation for intemperate attacks on anything its editors did not approve of. The Democrats and President Franklin D. Roosevelt were among its frequent targets. It would have been logical for the *Post* to attack Roosevelt for uprooting Japanese Americans, but logic did not always guide its actions. In this instance, it hated "Japs" even more than it hated F.D.R. It found a way to attack both targets when a former Heart Mountain employee—he turned out to be an illegal immigrant from Canada—who was fired for incompetence went to the *Post* with a wild story about food hoarding and waste at the camp. The *Post* sent its veteran hatchet man, Jack Carberry, to Heart Mountain to investigate the charges. With instructions to show Carberry whatever he wanted to see, I was among those who escorted him around the camp. As it turned out, it didn't matter what he saw. Carberry had been sent to Heart Mountain to write that WRA was pampering fat, lazy, insolent "Japs" with sumptuous meals while red-blooded Americans were suffering from food rationing. And that was exactly what he wrote.

The *Sentinel* battled back, but it was an unfair fight from the beginning. We had a circulation of 6,000, mostly internal. The Post printed something like 200,000 copies daily. We were a chihuahua yipping at a snarling rottweiler, but our readers loved it. Our readers were appreciative, too, that we made space available to a diversity of opinion. The Sentinel welcomed reader comment, whether it was in response to bigoted politicians or a coal shortage in the camp.

Despite being what amounted to a political prisoner in my own country, I was enjoying running the paper. Then one day in early 1943 distressing news came. Alice's mother, who was being held at an alien camp in Texas, wrote that a lump on the side of her neck had grown alarmingly, and doctors there had been unable to diagnose the problem. We wrote to the authorities, asking permission for her to seek outside medical help and suggesting the Mayo Clinic in Rochester, Minnesota. The authorities must have been worried about her condition because they granted permission for her to travel, unaccompanied, to the clinic. Because Mrs. Miyake spoke little English, Alice and I sought and received approval to meet her there without benefit of a government escort. Official policy had changed since we arrived at Heart Mountain. The government's concern now was to get the evacuees out of the camps as quickly as possible, and travel was being encouraged.

I had sufficient cash for train tickets to Minneapolis and enough in a Seattle bank to pay for the rest of the trip. But the bank check hadn't arrived by the time we had to leave for Billings to catch a Minnesota-bound train. No matter. Fortified by a combination of optimism and desperation, Alice, Mike, and I set out anyway, determined to manage. We simply could not let Alice's mother, ailing and confused, arrive alone in Rochester.

Near the depot in Billings, I looked up a little restaurant run by Mrs. Honkawa, a widow I had never met. What gave me the courage to approach her was that her son, Byron, had attended the University of Washington in Seattle and knew my brother. I introduced myself, told her of my problem, and asked for a loan, which I would pay back as soon as the money arrived from Seattle. She asked how much I needed. It was a fairly substantial sum for the time—round-trip rail fare for two to the Twin Cities, bus fare to Rochester, plus the cost of hotel and meals. Without hesitation, she went into a back room and emerged with a roll of greenbacks, which she placed my hands. I offered to sign a note. She said it wasn't necessary. It had taken a lot of beef stew, meat loaf and mashed potatoes, and coffee and doughnuts to put aside that kind of money.

From the depot in St. Paul, where the temperature was near zero, I telephoned Earl Tanbara, a refugee from Berkeley, and his wife Ruth, originally from Portland. They had moved inland to avoid the Evacuation and were spending a good deal of time helping people like us. Ruth was at work, but Earl invited us to his home for a bath and breakfast. Over coffee, I told him about Mrs. Honkawa. Earl didn't have much money, but he gave me enough to repay Mrs. Honkawa on the way back. People were like that in those times of adversity.

In Rochester, we found an inexpensive hotel and reached the depot in time to meet Mama. After two days of tests, the findings were not encouraging. She had a form of Hodgkin's disease, a cancer that resisted the treatment available in those days. She had, at most, two years to live. We put her on the train back to the Texas camp, promising to plead for her release to us in Heart Mountain.

It was a long trip back to Wyoming, broken only by a stop at Mrs. Honkawa's restaurant to repay the loan with Earl's money. The bank check was waiting at the camp, and we sent Earl a money order as soon as the post office opened for business. Several months later, Mrs. Miyake, no longer considered a security risk, was allowed to join us in Heart Mountain.

The army, which had been concerned only with getting Japanese Americans out of so-called sensitive areas, wasn't much interested in us after we were interned. We became the responsibility of WRA, which presumably would run the detention camps into the indefinite future. Almost from the beginning, WRA's leadership saw the injustice and folly—and potential legal liability—in keeping one group of Americans locked up in camps like so many prisoners of war. Dillon Myer quickly added to WRA's functions a "relocation" program under which internees were encouraged to leave the camps to find jobs and make homes in inland areas. WRA opened offices in Chicago, Cleveland, St. Louis, and other Midwestern cities to spread the gospel that Japanese Americans weren't subversives after all and to help locate jobs for them.

The Sentinel endorsed this program strongly and encouraged Heart Mountaineers to relocate before they stagnated in camp. But I hadn't thought seriously of personally becoming a relocatee. Hanging over my head was the old question as to whether any newspaper would hire me. Besides, I was enjoying running what in effect was my own publication. Three incidents helped me make up my mind to leave the camp as soon as possible.

One stifling midsummer day in 1943, about a year after entering the camp, I returned to our unit during a fierce dust storm. The wind was whipping up sand and gravel, so it was hazardous to be out in the open. I found Alice and Mike crouched under an umbrella at the entrance to our unit. "What are you doing out here?" I asked incredulously. Alice looked at me through red-rimmed eyes and said there was so much dust inside that it was almost impossible to breathe, and besides, it was intolerably hot in there. It was better, she said, to be outside in the dust storm with the umbrella to fend off the wind. I realized then that I had been so busy working, and enjoying my work, that I had paid little attention to my family's needs. Aside from the misery of making do in a barracks room, it must have been unspeakably boring for Alice, with nothing to do but baby-sit our son and wait for the mess hall gong to summon us to another dreary meal.

The second incident took place one day when I took Mike with me to Cody, where I had Sentinel business. Mike had spent more than half of his three years behind a barbed wire fence where the ground was either dusty or muddy. As we walked, he carefully avoided the lawns. I watched curiously until he pointed to the grass and asked what it was. "It's grass," I said. "You can walk on it. Take off your shoes and socks and try it." Cautiously, he tested the grass with his bare toes, feeling the soft coolness. Then he pushed himself out like a swimmer entering water. "It's grass, Daddy," he exulted. "You can walk on it! It feels good!" I started to laugh but was choked by a surge of anger. "No matter what the government thinks of me," I muttered, "it has no right to deny my son the pleasure of walking on grass any day he wants."

The third event was my mother-in-law's arrival in Heart Mountain. The medical care she could get there was inadequate. Periodically, she was taken to a hospital in Billings for radiation treatment. For the last months of her life, she deserved more than the bare comforts of camp life, more than mess hall food, more than sweltering heat and dust storms and a communal bathroom.

I told Bonnie Mechau it was time for me to make plans to leave. "I was wondering when you would say that," he responded.

Less than a month later, Bonnie told me I had been offered a job as a copyeditor at the *Register* in Des Moines, Iowa, and urged me to take it. I knew the *Register* had a good reputation, but I wondered where this opportunity had come from. And why Iowa? Bonnie said he understood that Myer, WRA's big boss, had taken a personal interest in my relocation. He had called Gardner (Mike) Cowles, who owned the *Register* and *Tribune* in Des Moines, *Look* magazine in New York, and other properties. Well, I told myself, if the people at the *Register* were willing to hire me on Myer's say-so, I'd show them I could handle the job.

Getting hired proved to be easier than getting out of the camp. Relocatees had to pass army, navy, and FBI scrutiny to be certified as "clean." Some of the information in their files identified me as "subversive." These charges, which I didn't learn about until decades later, must have held up my release. More than a month passed before WRA was given permission to let me go. Finally, early in October 1943, WRA gave us railroad tickets and $25 apiece—just like convicts leaving prison—and escorted us to the gate, where we caught the bus for Billings. Bonnie and the *Sentinel* staff were there to bid us good luck and good-bye. After seventeen months as prisoners of our own government, we were free, free, free. What a beautiful feeling that was.

Our first destination, significantly, was Independence, Missouri, a suburb of Kansas City, where my brother was working on a small weekly paper. I left my family with him and Yoshi while I went on ahead to Des

Moines to report for work and find a place to live. Quakers, kind and compassionate people, were running a hostel for us resettlers in a huge old house not far from downtown. We could rent a room and get a couple of meals for $1 a day while helping with the chores. There were eight or nine of us rooming there, and we would share tips about jobs, houses or rooms to rent, and how to get around town on the streetcar system. I spent ten days at the hostel before I finally found a place to rent.

I didn't know how I would be received at the *Register,* but the welcome was warm and sincere. My boss was Frank Eyerly, a sharp-eyed veteran newspaperman with uncanny instincts and extremely demanding standards. I learned a great deal about editing from him. My immediate boss was Ray Wright, perhaps ten years older than I, a thoroughly competent professional. My hours were 5 p.m. to 1 a.m.

My job as copyeditor involved reading material others had written, checking it for spelling, grammar, and accuracy, and putting a headline over it. But there was more. The *Register* had a system under which a copyeditor who came to work in midafternoon skimmed through all the material then available for the next morning's paper. This material, called copy, was separated according to subject and placed in "books," which were simply sheets of paper folded in two.

Ray Wright would examine the books and distribute them among the copyeditors, who sat on the rim of a large, circular desk. If, for example, Congress had taken action on a certain bill, the pertinent book might contain up-to-date stories on the situation provided by Associated Press and United Press, a report from the *Register*'s Washington staff, plus copies of earlier stories providing useful background information. "Give me the best fourteen inches on Congress, and put a No. 2 head on it," Wright might say. The copyeditor would then study the material in the book and assemble a story fourteen inches long that would give the reader a comprehensive and interesting account of what Congress had decided on that particular issue. Then he would write a headline of the specified size and style.

Sometimes the Associated Press story would be well-organized and complete, needing nothing more. Sometimes it might require only the insertion of a sentence or a paragraph or two from other sources to improve it. On other occasions, the copyeditor would write the entire story using the raw material in the book. This kind of work had to be done quickly and required skill and background. Each copyeditor had his specialties. For example, the man handling the war in Europe would be assigned the main war story every night. I, the newest and least experienced member of the copy desk staff, at first was given the odds and ends and routine stories about petty crimes, minor court cases, and the other everyday grist for the newspaper's mill.

After a week or so, it was evident to Wright and Eyerly that I could do the job, and gradually I was given more important stories to handle. My starting salary was $35 a week. Wartime regulations limited pay increases, but every three or four months, my pay was increased by $2.50.

Finding a house to rent was the hardest part of settling in Des Moines. There simply weren't any. Eventually, I located a run-down two-story house in an old part of the city. It was not far from a streetcar line that ran every hour after midnight, an important consideration, given my work schedule. I quickly signed a lease, and only then did the rest of the family come up from Missouri (I was able to repay my brother's kindness in housing Alice and Mike by recommending him for a job at the *Register,* and he, too, moved to Des Moines). We discovered during the first winter that the house was like a sieve; the unrelenting Iowa wind blew through it at will, and on the worst days the hand-fired coal-burning furnace was unable to keep the temperature comfortable. It was like being back in Heart Mountain, except there was little dust, and on my days off, we were free to board the streetcar and go wherever we wished.

My night hours made it possible for me to do most of the marketing. Every few days, I'd take the streetcar downtown to the public market and return with two shopping bags of groceries. A butcher and I became friendly, and he would help me stretch the supply of red ration coupons necessary to buy meat.

Alice had been pregnant with our second child when we left Heart Mountain. The baby was due March 1, 1944. On February 29, I went to work as usual. When I came home after midnight, Grandma said Alice had called a taxi from Eisentraut's drugstore on the corner—we had been unable to get a telephone because of wartime shortages—and gone to the hospital. There was no way to call a cab. I hurried back to the streetcar line in time to catch the trolley making its return trip downtown, transferred to another streetcar, and went to the hospital. Alice had just gone into labor, but it appeared the baby wouldn't be born for a while. By then I was nearly as exhausted as she. Alice insisted that I go home and get some sleep.

Early next morning, I walked up to Eisentraut's, called the hospital, and learned the baby—a girl we planned to name Susan—had been born a short while earlier. Mike and I took the streetcar to meet the newest member of the family.

With a new baby and an ailing grandmother in the family, it wouldn't do to spend another winter in the house. Rentals were still scarce. We finally found a two-bedroom cottage for sale. The price was $3,500, and my brother Bob loaned me the money for part of the down payment.

Ronald Lynam, a textbook salesman, and his wife Pauline lived next door. They were somewhat alarmed when they learned a "Japanese" family was moving in. Pauline called the WRA office and asked some questions. When we moved in, we found our front lawn newly mowed. It was the Lynams' way of welcoming their new neighbors, and that introduction led to a warm friendship. When Mama died, almost two years after her visit to the Mayo Clinic, Pauline pitched in like a member of the family to help with the arrangements. The Red Cross notified Kenny, who was with the 442nd Regiment somewhere in Europe, but of course he couldn't come back for the services. My mother-in-law was cremated, so her ashes could be taken back to the West Coast someday.

We were also developing other friendships, mainly through the newspaper. Ole Hellie, an expert copyeditor, and his wife Elizabeth lived a few blocks away. Both were interested in music, the classics, and international affairs, and we visited them often. Jerry Thrailkill, the Register's farm editor, lived on an acreage about a mile away, and he let me use some of his land to grow sweet corn, tomatoes, and other vegetables. Mike made friends with the Moore kids who lived down the street. It was a pleasant enough situation, and even after war's end, when we were free to return to Seattle, I would have been happy to remain in Des Moines.

But we could not deny our longing to return to the West. We missed the mountains and the smell of salt water. We disliked the hot and humid summers that produced bumper crops of corn and soybeans, and the frigid storms that swept down from the northern prairies. Besides, we knew we had to find some relief for Mike from the allergies that plagued him in spring and summer.

In the spring of 1946, I read a small item in *Time* magazine about the death of a brilliant young painter named Frank Mechau. Frank was Bonnie's brother. I wrote Bonnie a brief note expressing my condolences, and eventually Bonnie replied. Among the things he told me was that the *Denver Post,* the paper we had tilted with through the *Sentinel,* had a new publisher named Palmer Hoyt who was rebuilding the staff and generally shaking things up. He had been publisher of the Portland *Oregonian* and had a reputation as a liberal. Bonnie urged me to write to Hoyt for a job, which I did.

Some weeks later, I received a telegram from Hoyt's managing editor. He offered me a job as copyeditor at $60 a week. I was making $62.50 at the *Register.* The salary cut didn't bother me, but suddenly I was filled with doubts. I couldn't stomach working for a vicious, unscrupulous paper such as I had known the *Post* to be while at Heart Mountain. Could one man change a leopard's spots? I had to find out. I wrote Hoyt for an interview, and after work one night, I caught a train for Denver. Next morning, after washing up in the men's room at the depot, I went to see him.

He was a chunky man with hands like a blacksmith and a deep rumbling voice. He listened quietly to my concerns, then assured me the old *Post* was no more. He told me he wanted me to join his staff and help him make the newspaper one we could be proud of, that I would go as far on the paper as my abilities would take me. We shook hands on that.

Eyerly asked me to stay. He even offered another $2.50 raise, with more to come as soon as wartime regulations were removed. It was nice to be wanted, but Alice and I had made up our minds that we were going back West.

Getting there proved to be as difficult as the original trip to Iowa. A Chevrolet dealer had been promising me a car out of his next shipment from the newly reopened assembly lines, but somehow the automobile never materialized. I suspected the new cars were going to customers willing to pay something extra under the table. Finally the day came for moving out of our home, and still there was no car. Even if reservations had been available, taking the two children and all our luggage by train would have been a daunting challenge. In desperation I explored the used car lots, where there were nothing but weary prewar clunkers, and finally settled on what seemed to be a serviceable Hudson sedan. The paint was shot and the chassis leaned a little to one side, but what the heck, it was roomy, and the motor was steady.

Loaded down like the Joads in Steinbeck's *The Grapes of Wrath,* we headed for Seattle, where my family would stay while I scouted for a house in Denver. My choice in used cars didn't turn out to be entirely disastrous, but it wasn't good, either. We had to stop in Broken Bow, Nebraska, to replace the generator. In Denver, the rear end had to be overhauled. In Medicine Bow, Wyoming, a wobbly wheel had to be replaced.

As we drove up our street in Des Moines for the last time, Susan, who was just learning to speak in sentences, looked back and said in a small, mournful voice, "I have no home."

Des Moines, the *Register* and my colleagues there, the Lynams, and a lot of wonderful Iowa folk had been good to this family of reluctant refugees. It was hard to leave the real America we had come to know.

Chapter Four

Hosokawa of the *Post*

The newsroom of the *Denver Post,* on the second floor of an ancient building on Champa Street, was in semi-chaos when I reported for work on July 15, 1946. Old-timers, unable or unwilling to meet Palmer Hoyt's standards, were quitting. Newcomers like me showed up unexpectedly. There didn't seem to be enough chairs for all the employees. Al Birch, the promotion director, who spent much of his time out of the office, chained his chair to his desk so it wouldn't disappear in his absence.

Newspaper people fall into two basic categories. First there are the reporters who gather and write the news. They are out of the office much of the time. And then there are the editors who sit at a desk and evaluate what the reporters have written, edit the material, and undertake the mechanical process of finding a place for it in the newspaper. I had been hired as a copyeditor, which meant my primary job was to edit what others had written.

Larry Martin, the acerbic managing editor, had told me I would be assigned as a reporter at the cop shop—the police station—for the first two weeks so I could become acquainted with Denver preparatory to taking on editing chores. Martin was out sick when I reported for work. Jim Hale, who was sitting in as managing editor, said, "Never mind what Mr. Martin told you, the paper is hurting for copyeditors. Take off your coat, find a chair and pick up a pencil, and go to work." And that's what I did.

A few weeks later, I was made swing man—that is, I filled in for any editor who had the day off. One day, I put together page one; the next day, I was a wire editor, reading all the dispatches that Associated Press and other services sent in from around the world and selecting the material to print in the paper. A third day, I handled the regional news page. Then I would work as a slot man, supervising the copy desk, where stories were edited and headlines written. If Hoyt was testing me, he was giving me a workout.

But another man was watching me, too—William Shepherd. He had been publisher until replaced by Hoyt, and as Frederick G. Bonfils's successor, had directed the *Post* through some of its most flamboyant and rambunctious years. Now, as a courtesy to this aging and rejected leader, he had been given a desk in the newsroom. In reality it was more an insult than a courtesy. Shepherd had nothing to do and no privacy in which to do it. Bewildered by the changes, he seemed to spend much of his time staring at the new employees, mostly me. He did not speak once to me in the months before he quit coming to the office.

One of Hoyt's early moves was to start up a Sunday magazine that would reflect the spirit of the region. In that its format was limited to eight nearly full-size newspaper pages, it wasn't really a magazine. But it was printed in rotogravure in Chicago, which permitted use of vivid color pictures, and it had enough space to give magazine treatment to stories about Western people, history, and attractions. Hoyt's intention was to eventually install the *Post*'s own rotogravure printing plant and publish a "real" magazine. Elvon Howe, who had a flair for writing, returned from naval service and was chosen to edit the new section, which was called *Rocky Mountain Empire Magazine*. After a few months of indoctrination in the newsroom, I was named Howe's assistant. My job involved selecting and editing material to be published, supervising layout, and doing some writing of my own. It was a good assignment in that it gave me the opportunity to travel throughout Colorado and adjoining states in search of story material, become acquainted with the mountains and high plains, and meet a variety of interesting people. Only twice, over a long span of years as a newspaperman, did my race seem to concern anyone.

One day in Liberal, Kansas, Jim Cinnamon, publisher of the local *Southwest Daily Times,* took me around town for an hour, then left while I went to the motel to wash up. When I saw Cinnamon later for dinner, he said, "At least a dozen people wanted to know who you are. Some of them said, 'Hey, Jim, who's your Chinese friend?' I told them you're the *Denver Post* reporter. That's all they wanted to know." After a pause, Cinnamon asked, "Say, what are you, anyway?"

Among the people I met, there was only casual curiosity about my race. The *Denver Post* was well-known, and anybody from the paper commanded respect and attention, if not fear lingering from the old days.

Another time, I had gone to Spearfish, South Dakota, to speak at a writers' conference at the local college. No one seemed to think it strange that someone with a Japanese name and face had come to help them improve their English writing skills. After I had spoken, a dear old lady came up to me and asked how my name was spelled. I showed her the name tag on my lapel and spelled it out for her. "Oh, yes," she responded. "A very unusual name. Is it Polish?" The only thing I could think to say was, "No, ma'am, it isn't Polish. Do you think I look Polish?" I had been mistaken for a Chinese and an Indian but never for a Slav. I wondered whether the little old lady was simply befuddled or, isolated in the Black Hills, had she been so completely insulated from the shifting currents of American life that she could not distinguish a Japanese face from that of any other "foreigner," in this case a Pole. Or was she such a democratic cosmopolite that her eyes did not register whether a person's skin was black, brown, white, or yellow?

If my race aroused no more than mild, friendly curiosity in the boondocks, it did cause something of a fuss when I tried to buy a home in the lower-middle-class Park Hill area of Denver. Our third child, a son we named Peter, was born on May 29, 1948, and we needed a larger home. Alice and I found a small, three-bedroom brick bungalow with a neatly tended yard, not far from a grade school. The realtor took Alice and me through the house, but when we went back to his office to discuss details, he abruptly said he could not sell it to us. Under prodding, he made it clear that since the house was in an all-white area, his firm had an obligation to protect the neighborhood.

All right, I thought, if that's how it was, we'd look elsewhere, but not before I made him and his boss uncomfortable with some pointed comments. As we scouted around, it became obvious that other realtors were bound by the same discriminatory practice. We finally found a house we liked with a "For Sale by Owner" sign in front of it. The owner turned out to be a noncommissioned air force officer who was more interested in selling his property and getting out of town than in upholding a racist housing practice.

But our move did occasion some hostility. The couple next door did not take kindly to the idea of having us for neighbors. Alerted by Howe to this unfortunate state of affairs, some of my co-workers decided a show of support was appropriate. They rounded up cases of beer and mounds of victuals, and more than fifty of them showed up on a Sunday afternoon for an all-American housewarming party that demonstrated in rousing fashion to the entire neighborhood that we had friends. I couldn't help but wonder what would have happened in the early days of 1942 if Caucasians on the West Coast had rallied to our support in a similar fashion.

On June 25, 1950, Communist North Korea, misreading American resolve for keeping the peace, invaded South Korea. Columns of crack troops spearheaded by Russian-built tanks seized the capital, Seoul, almost without resistance. Three days after the outbreak, my fourth child and second daughter, Christie, was born. In Korea, U.S. troops were thrown into combat, but, soft from Occupation duty in Japan, they were no match for the invaders. City after city fell to the North Koreans as long lines of refugees fled south. It looked as though the mighty United States, the world's greatest military power five years earlier, was about to get the hell kicked out of it.

We were discussing the war one day in the newsroom when I said casually that I had traveled over some of the area where U.S. troops were now in bitter, bloody retreat. "That's awfully rugged country to be fighting a war in," I remember saying. "Lots of steep mountains and narrow valleys cut up into rice paddies. No roads to speak of. No space to maneuver."

A few days later, Hoyt called me into his office. "I hear you want to go to Korea to cover the war," he said. In fact, I hadn't said anything of the kind, but I told Hoyt that if he wanted to send me, I thought I could do a decent job. "I know you could," Hoyt said. "If you want to go, we want you to go. You'll be the *Post*'s first war correspondent."

Today I'm not sure why I decided to take the assignment. I was thirty-five years old, comfortable in a desk job. My wife Alice and I had four children—Mike, who was not quite ten; Susan, who was six; Pete, who was two; and Christie, less than a month old. We had moved only recently into a house that needed a lot of work. We had a car, but Alice had never learned to drive. The nearest supermarket was many blocks away. Alice and I agonized over my decision. Ultimately, we agreed that after all we'd been through, it wasn't wise to turn down a professional opportunity. A month after the outbreak of war, I was on my way to see what the situation in Korea was all about.

First stop, Tokyo, still threadbare, still struggling to recover from the devastation of defeat, still very much aware of the presence of American Occupation forces. I was there only long enough to pick up correspondent's credentials and combat fatigues, establish lines of communication back to Denver, and look up some old friends before heading for Taegu, South Korea, where the U.S. military effort was headquartered. It was a weary, dusty, sunburned town not far from the winding Naktong River, which American and Allied forces had established as the last line of defense. If that line were breached, the Allies would be driven off the Korean Peninsula.

The correspondents were billeted in an old two-story schoolhouse near the center of town. We slept on cots in a common room on the second floor and ate breakfast, comprised invariably of reconstituted eggs, canned sausage, toast, and coffee, in a mess hall on the first floor. Then, in search of exciting stories, we scattered for the day. When we returned in the evening, we took cold showers using a hose in the schoolyard. This life was luxurious compared to the way the troops lived; we could come back to relative safety and shelter when it became dark. The G.I.s who weren't out on patrol or engaged in a firefight slept on the ground surrounded by the terrors of the night. From the schoolhouse, we could see flashes of artillery fire on distant hills and fell asleep to the rumble of cannon.

My strategy was to hitchhike to as many front-line command posts as possible and seek out men from Colorado, Wyoming, Nebraska, Kansas, South Dakota, and New Mexico—the *Post*'s circulation area—for stories on "local" boys. The wire service reporters could cover the big picture—for example, which division gained or lost how many hundred yards while killing how many of the enemy. I wrote about visiting with Private First Class Joe Gonzales, a rifleman whose folks worked on a sugar beet farm near Sterling, Colorado; told what Joe was doing, how he lived, and how he felt about the lousy mess that was Korea; and sent his family his love. There were countless men to be interviewed during the day and endless stories to be written at night about the sights and sounds and smells of a savage war. And letters to be written home to Alice and the kids.

Early in September, when I had flown back to Tokyo for a few days of rest, hot showers, a haircut, and decent food, I heard rumors of a major operation about to take shape. The navy, I heard, would be involved. I headed for Sasebo, the big U.S. base on Kyushu, the southernmost of Japan's main islands. A public information officer secured me a berth on the *Valley Forge,* a giant aircraft carrier commissioned in the final days of World War II. There I found a whole new world. A small but comfortable cabin of my own. Laundry service. An officers' wardroom where meals were served on linen and china by waiters, not out of a can, and where ice cream and coffee were always available. A PX sold candy bars, snacks, recent magazines, and all manner of other things. The ship was a huge, self-contained city that was home for several thousand men. I busied myself looking for and interviewing sailors from the mountain states.

Each morning at first light, the *Valley Forge* would launch jets, as well as propeller planes, that disappeared over the horizon and then, like homing pigeons, found their way back after a couple of hours. We were patrolling the Yellow Sea, between China and the Korean Peninsula, and would be supporting an amphibious landing at Inchon, the port of Seoul, which was in Communist hands.

D-Day was September 15, 1950, my brother's birthday. They woke me up early, strapped on a parachute, showed me which D-ring to pull in case I had to jump, and stuffed me into what amounted to the jump seat of a Skyraider dive-bomber. The Skyraider was a brute, a single-engine propeller-driven plane as heavy as a DC-3 airliner, armed with rockets, 500-pound bombs, and rapid-fire 20-millimeter cannon that spit out streams of banana-sized projectiles. There was only a single seat in the cockpit for the pilot, but in a few models there was a seat for an observer to the side of and slightly above the pilot's cockpit. The observer could see only to the right through a narrow window. That's where I sat in the formation's lead plane, piloted by a stocky, muscular lieutenant commander named Norman Hodson.

The terror of the mission is still with me. From a dead stop, the plane was catapulted to flying speed within the length of the carrier's deck. The sudden acceleration pinned me back into the seat as though a giant ram had been jammed against my chest. My eyeballs felt as though they were being thrust through the back of my skull. As the plane leveled off, I heard Hodson asking through the intercom, "You all right?" I groaned.

The squadron, with Hodson in the lead, headed inland, flying low over burned-out villages, burned skeletons of trucks on dirt roads, and burned hulks of tanks with impotent cannon barrels protruding at stark angles. Occasionally, Hodson spoke to me over the intercom, pointing out bridges, barracks, trucks, and railroad cars knocked out in earlier strikes. Suddenly, he spotted what appeared to be eight rectangular haystacks at the foot of a steep hill just off the dirt road we were following.

I heard the pilot's voice: "Sometimes they hide tanks under those haystacks. Just to make sure, we're going to take them. You're going to hear a thump. Don't worry. It always makes that noise when I cut a bomb loose."

He circled once, then nosed over and headed down, down, down. Only hundreds of feet from the ground, I heard the jarring thump of a bomb being released, and he pulled up sharply. This time, I was jammed down into the seat, and my eyeballs felt as though they were about to fall into my lap. I managed to look out and saw a huge puff of flame and billowing black smoke. Circling back above the fire, we could see other planes from our squadron peeling off in long steep glides, dropping their bombs, and pulling out as flame and smoke repeatedly blossomed below. Hodson made three more runs, sometimes plummeting to an altitude of barely twenty feet, strafing the targets with his cannon, before he was satisfied. As we pulled away, all eight "haystacks" were burning fiercely. "Got some," the pilot muttered with satisfaction.

A few moments later, we made another run at some twenty trucks and what appeared to be weapons carriers parked alongside a barracks area near the burned-out city of Taejon. We made a series of ground-level passes at the targets, blasting away with rockets. To my right, I could see two other planes from our formation diving along with us. Rockets under their wings took off in a flash of flame, trailing smoke as they sped toward the trucks. Then again came the wrenching agony of the pullout.

Hodson hadn't fired the cannon for a while, but he took care of that shortly. "To the right," he said. "See where the rails go into that tunnel in the mountain? See the wisps of smoke coming out of the tunnel? I bet they've hidden a locomotive in there. I'm going to give them a few rounds."

He headed straight for the mountain, firing bursts into the tunnel's mouth. When would he pull up? I froze, ready for the crash into the mountainside, when he pulled away with a thunderous roar and headed almost straight up. The sky was clear, and far off was the Yellow Sea, blue and placid. Somewhere out there was the *Valley Forge,* awaiting our return. Eventually, my guts and eyeballs and other body parts returned to their normal positions. "This guy," I said to myself, "does this for a living. He does it every day. And he enjoys it. And so does every man in his unit." I saluted him silently.

We were now over the ocean, and long lines of cruisers and destroyers were escorting landing ships toward the Inchon beaches. Shortly, Marines would be going ashore to secure beachheads. After everything we had been through that morning, finding our ship and landing on what appeared to be a stamp-sized deck was a cinch.

Two days later, the navy delivered me to Kimpo Airfield on Seoul's outskirts. The place was buzzing with cargo carriers. North Korean dead still lay where they had fallen. In a bean field at the edge of the airfield was the uniformed body of a boy perhaps no more than fifteen or sixteen years old, sprawled on his back. The top of his skull had been blown off, and fluid from his brain had oozed into the soil. I turned away, found correspondents I had known in Taegu, and we began the long walk toward the ruins of Seoul, which the Communists had abandoned after only a brief fight.

The end run General MacArthur's strategists had devised cleverly bypassed the massed North Korean troops who had pinned Allied forces on the southern tip of the peninsula. In danger of being cut off from their bases in the north, the Communists were racing for home. Seoul was recaptured, and the war appeared to have been won. In mid-October,

I received a cablegram from Ed Dooley, the *Post*'s managing editor, saying it was time to return to Denver and take on a new assignment—editor of the new *Sunday Empire Magazine* launched by Howe, who had the misfortune of being called back into naval service.

Alice met me at the airport and proudly drove me home. She had taken lessons in my absence and learned to drive the Chevy as a matter of self-preservation, even though some of the neighbors had been very kind about taking her shopping. The kids had grown wondrously even during three short months. But I scarcely had time to enjoy my family before I was summoned to the office and brought up to date on the struggling new magazine. Hoyt's orders were brief: put out the best damned magazine possible.

I knew how to write magazine-style, which is substantially different from newspaper-style. Writing for a magazine requires a flair, a storytelling skill, and an eye and ear for detail that many excellent daily reporters never develop. But the problem was that I had little experience assembling the exact mix of reading material—one that included variety and change of tone, pace, and subject matter from one story to the next—that makes a good magazine. With a free hand, I learned by trial and error.

One of the magazine's goals was to encourage regional freelance writers. But I soon discovered that most of the material we were buying was so far below my standards that extensive rewriting was required. It made no sense to pay money for manuscripts and then pay a staff writer to rewrite them. So I gradually built up a staff that could be depended on to produce first-class copy. In time, thanks to a talented and dedicated team, *Empire* became one of the best—some were kind enough to call it the best—of the forty or fifty Sunday newspaper magazines then being published.

My early efforts to create a magazine were interrupted by unexpected demands on my time. Today, the Korean police action is a somewhat forgotten war. But back then, there was intense interest in Korea, the significance of our involvement, and news about our men on distant battlefields. My stories from Korea had been very well read, and Coloradans were anxious to learn more. I received dozens of invitations to speak at service clubs, schools, and church groups, and the newspaper urged me to accept as many as possible because it created good public relations for the *Post*. In the months after my return, I spoke before more than 100 audiences throughout Colorado. It was a great way to get to know the people of the state, but it was rough on family life and wreaked havoc with my forty-hour work week. When the Communist Chinese entered the war in Korea and United Nations forces (meaning Americans) were once more in retreat, I felt sympathy for the dogfaces but had no wish to be with them. There was too much to do on the home front, and I had had enough of war for a while.

But I could not avoid it forever. In 1964, the Post sent me back to Southeast Asia—this time, to Vietnam. At that point, we had 20,000 American troops, mostly career soldiers, in the country as "military advisers." Their morale was high because they felt they were engaged in something useful: their mission was to train South Vietnamese government troops to protect the country from the aggressive Communist North Vietnamese. In order to maintain our dubious status as noncombatants, Americans had orders not to fire until fired upon. All of that was to change shortly after the so-called Tonkin Incident when the North Vietnamese allegedly fired on American warships. The United States then took over the responsibility of defending South Vietnam with hundreds of thousands of troops. They were mostly young draftees—poorly trained, poorly disciplined Americans who did not understand the Vietnamese, feared the jungle, and hated the country and climate—whose primary goal was to survive the eleven-month tour of duty and go home. Who could blame them?

One night, I went out on a helicopter mission arranged for me by Captain George Young, whose wife lived in Colorado Springs. The nature of the mission severely tested the "don't fire until fired upon" order. Three Huey helicopters were involved. The first flew low over trees shading the maze of waterways in the Mekong Delta, turning on its spotlights frequently in search of Vietcong encampments. In reality it was a decoy, inviting ground fire. The second Huey, completely dark, flew slightly behind and above the lead aircraft, with gunners ready to cut loose a retaliatory hail of bombs and bullets the moment the Vietcong began shooting. I was in the third helicopter, hovering above the other two, waiting to witness the unfolding of this grim drama and prepared to dive in to rescue the crewmen if one of the other helicopters went down. On that night, nothing untoward happened.

Another day, I rode on a supply mission to a Special Forces outpost on a low, isolated mountain peak. A handful of Green Berets were stationed there with 100 or more Hmong tribesmen and their families. Their mission was to track Vietcong activity and disrupt them whenever possible. It was a lonely outpost surrounded by hostiles and linked to the rest of the world only by radio and helicopter.

Wherever I went, it was evident our mission in Vietnam was to help the people establish a viable nation without Communist harassment. I was able to witness some fine Americans engaged in that effort. But somewhere along the way, something went awry. The war became our war, hated by the soldiers and opposed by the people at home, and I don't think we've recovered fully from the trauma that followed.

I had been editor of *Empire* Magazine for six years when Ed Dooley, the thoroughly respected managing editor, left the *Post* to found a business journal in San Francisco. Hoyt picked Mort Stern, a bright writer who only recently had returned to the paper from a year as Niemann Fellow at Harvard, as his new managing editor. And although I had not known him well, Stern asked me to be his assistant.

The next four years, first under Stern and later Bob Lucas, were among the most interesting, and demanding, of my career. The managing editor's primary responsibility was to think the big thoughts and keep the publisher happy and out of trouble. His assistant saw to it that an exciting, accurate, newsy, bright, complete newspaper was produced on time every day. I do not recall which requirement was most important. It may have been punctuality, because the minute the last page, usually page one, was assembled and sent to the stereotypers was recorded meticulously. If there were too many late pages, the production people complained to the business office, which complained to the managing editor, who bucked the problem to the assistant managing editor. But there was undeniable excitement in supervising—others did the actual work—the content and appearance of a newspaper read daily by hundreds of thousands of subscribers. It never seemed to occur to anyone that the fellow in shirtsleeves overseeing all this had once been confined behind a barbed wire fence because his government believed his ethnicity made him a potential national security risk.

Bob Lucas left in 1960, and Bill Hornby, an editorial writer from Montana, was named managing editor. He picked his own assistant, and

I was given the largely honorary title of Sunday editor. I was back in charge of *Empire Magazine* but had a variety of other duties, including some heavy-duty writing assignments. Among them was the aborted summit in Paris where Nikita Khrushchev gave President Eisenhower a bad time over the Gary Powers incident, Powers being the pilot of the U–2 spy plane that had been shot down over Russia.

I was only in Paris because the *Post,* like all but the largest and wealthiest newspapers of that time, didn't let principle stand in the way of saving a buck. A French shipping line had scheduled the launching of a huge luxury liner, and a number of American travel writers were invited to witness the event, all expenses paid. Bruce Hamby, the *Post's* travel editor, had been invited, but he wasn't interested and offered me the opportunity to go in his place. The launching was in Brest, not far from Paris, where the summit would be held a few days later. Why not pop in on the summit while I had a free ride to the neighborhood?

The summit adjourned early when President Eisenhower declined to apologize for sending U–2 planes over the Soviet Union on spying missions. But I was responsible for a minor international near-incident of my own. Some of us journalists, in the absence of anything newsworthy to report on, were standing outside the Soviet Embassy waiting for Khrushchev to appear. Presently, a black limousine drove up, and out jumped two large, red-faced men. One was Alexei Adzhubei, editor of Pravda and Khrushchev's son-in-law. He saw me, approached in what I interpreted as a menacing manner, and shouted something in Russian. I smiled weakly.

"He's asking your nationality," whispered Eddy Gilmore, the long-time Associated Press correspondent in Moscow. Then, in Russian, Eddy explained I was an American of Japanese ancestry. Adzhubei's scowl was replaced by a big grin. He thrust out a huge paw in a handshake and told Eddy he had thought I was one of Chiang Kai-shek's anti-Communist lackeys from Taiwan. Eddy wrote about this little episode, and the Associated Press put the story on its wire. When I returned to Denver, I found Eddy's story had run on the front page.

A few weeks later, I was on my way to Japan to cover another situation involving President Eisenhower. The Japanese government had rammed a renewal of the U.S.-Japan Mutual Security Treaty through Parliament, and the leftists were outraged. Left-wing students staged a series of massive demonstrations that threatened the government, and Eisenhower canceled his trip to Japan. Bob Lucas figured the reason for the fuss wasn't being explained adequately and instructed me to find out what was really going on and why. This time there was no shipping line to pay my fare. Lucas telephoned editors of nineteen other leading newspapers and got each of them to commit to one-twentieth of the cost of sending me to Tokyo in return for the right to publish my findings.

Parts of Tokyo were in turmoil. Each night, tens of thousands of radical students under the direction of an organization called Zengakuren chanted slogans and snake-danced through downtown streets, paralyzing traffic and calling for Prime Minister Nobusuke Kishi's head. One night, I watched more than 100,000 students demonstrating outside the iron gates in front of the Parliament building as riot police stood guard. But when I walked to the back of the building, there was no one to be seen, and I found no fence. Only a low hedge that any agile student could jump over separated the grounds from the street. The demonstrators could have invaded the building at any time, but none did. Their purpose was only to create a fuss where the television cameras were stationed. Some of them told me they weren't quite sure why they were demonstrating, except that they had been promised a free meal by leftist agitators if they showed up. Two decades later, I frequently would meet conservative business leaders in dark suits, dark ties, and white shirts who admitted they had been among the radical antigovernment demonstrators in 1960.

Elsewhere in Tokyo, life went on as usual. During the demonstrations, one of the TV channels carried professional baseball games. The bar and nightclub area, only a few blocks from the Parliament building, was jammed. During the day, when there was no sign of demonstrating students, I interviewed some of Japan's leading social commentators, academicians, and businessmen to seek an understanding of what was going on.

Apparently, my writing was beginning to be noticed outside Colorado. One day, a New Yorker named Hy Kellick got in touch with me. To call him a literary agent would be an aggrandizement. But he had contacts with a number of magazines, and he offered me an assignment to write a piece for *Pageant* about what a great place Colorado is. I think they paid me $400. Kellick took $40 as his agent's fee. Rearing four growing children on a *Post* salary wasn't easy. I took more assignments from Kellick and spent many nights writing for him. At first, most of the assignments were from men's action magazines, which were looking for vividly written copy about cops and robbers and derring-do based on real-life incidents but without much regard for accuracy. I wasn't proud of this work and wrote under a variety of pseudonyms, earning $125 to $150 per story—the equivalent of a week's pay at the *Post*. Ultimately, I was able to hit top markets like the old *Saturday Evening Post* and *Reader's Digest* with stories that were outside *Empire*'s field of interest. Such sales made feeding my family much easier. But the greatest satisfaction was the knowledge that my work was good enough to be bought by the biggest magazines in the country. Eventually, I turned my extracurricular writing to books and have nine to my credit.

In 1974 an official from the Consulate General of Japan in San Francisco called on me. He said that although Colorado was within the area served by his office, Denver was a long way from the coast, and in view of the growing commercial and cultural ties between that state and Japan, it seemed appropriate to open an honorary consulate here. Then he asked whether I would accept an appointment as unpaid honorary consul.

There was a long silence, and he felt it necessary to repeat the question. I didn't know what to say. Yes, I was of Japanese parentage and I was interested in that country. But Japan's perfidy had plunged my country into war and led to my imprisonment in an American-style concentration camp. Did I want to represent a foreign nation, particularly Japan? And if I did, how would it affect my position at the newspaper, where I was expected to be completely objective? There were many questions to ask and many people to talk to.

Alice encouraged me to accept. My boss Hoyt thought it was a nice honor and urged me to take the appointment—with the proviso that I not write any controversial material about Japan, although I would be free to express my opinion in staff editorial conferences. Just to be sure I was on safe ground, I talked to the U.S. district attorney and the head of the Denver FBI office. They assured me Japan was now a valued ally and the State Department had no objection to U.S. citizens taking honorary consular positions with friendly countries. Finally, I talked to Ben Stapleton, a Denver attorney who was the honorary French consul and dean of the Colorado Consular Corps, which comprised about twenty Denverites representing various countries. Only then did I agree to accept the appointment. If my precautions appear excessive, this was due to my unforgettable internment experience decades earlier. Japan now has seven or eight honorary consuls general in various parts of the United States, and I rank among the most senior. The work involved has been minimal and the duties interesting, and I have not regretted taking the position.

In 1977 the Post underwent another of its periodic staff shakeups and Bill Hornby was promoted from managing editor to editor. Bob Pattridge was named managing editor, and I was invited to take over his former position as editor of the editorial page. It was just about the only top job at the newspaper I hadn't held, and the prospect was exciting. Perhaps the greatest significance of my appointment was that I—someone who had been warned that he would never be employed by a newspaper because of his race—was being placed in charge of the opinion section of a large and influential daily paper. No one seemed upset that I would be responsible for expressing that newspaper's position on local, state, national, and international affairs, social and educational issues, the latest congressional blunder, and almost everything else.

As Lewis Carroll so appropriately put it,

> The time [had] come, the walrus said,
> to talk of many things,
> Of shoes and ships and sealing wax,
> of cabbages and kings.
> Any why the sea is boiling hot
> and whether pigs have wings.

Well, the "head walrus," had given me the job of talking to our readers about these shoes and ships, if not about winged pigs. With the support of a knowledgeable staff headed by a remarkably able assistant named Carole Green, I occupied the editorial page editor's corner office for seven years without getting either myself or the newspaper in serious trouble. I would like to believe the Post's opinion section during that time was interesting, illuminating, and provocative, perhaps just a bit left of center, but always thoughtful and fair. The publisher and I seemed to agree on most issues. Not once was I told to take a position that was contrary to my personal beliefs.

Then one day in 1983, the *Post*'s new owners told me it was time to go. I was sixty-eight years old and in no position to argue, but I had too much energy to hang 'em up.

Even without my job at the *Post,* I had plenty to keep me occupied. Before long, I was commuting each week to the University of Wyoming in Laramie, where I taught classes in magazine and editorial writing. The journalism school was in such turmoil that even I was offered the deanship on the suggestion that I had the background and prestige, if you will, to bring order to the department. I had virtually no academic background, but I found teaching satisfying. Yet I could see all manner of bear traps in a position that involved more administrating than educating and said thank you, but no.

In 1985, I had a call from Ralph Looney, editor of the *Rocky Mountain News.* He told me his readers' representative was leaving and asked whether I'd be interested in the position. Over lunch, he explained that the readers' representative was an ombudsman, a mediator between the newspaper and the public. When a reader had some complaint or comment about the newspaper's performance, he or she could write to the representative and get an answer. The readers' rep was responsible to no one and had direct access to any member of the staff. Though the job sounded interesting and required considerable knowledge of newspaper operations, I hesitated. The *Post* and the *News* were locked in a perennial circulation war, and going over to the "enemy" struck me as disloyal. But old friends told me that the *Post,* which had undergone two ownership changes, was no longer the newspaper I had served for so long. I took the position and spent several days a week for the next seven years pontificating about newspaper practices, chiding *News* staffers for errors, and trying to explain to readers how boo-boos slipped into the paper despite extensive precautions and why our business seemed guilty of a lot of foolishness.

Seven years of this work was enough. I retired permanently—but not entirely—in 1992.

"From the Frying Pan," the column I had been writing for the *Pacific Citizen* since 1942, was still alive, if not altogether well. I continued to write the column each week—and later every other week when financial problems forced *Pacific Citizen* to adopt a biweekly schedule. The column's character had changed over the years as both author and the readership, to put it kindly, matured. As I have mentioned, the best of "From the Frying Pan" had been collected in a book published with moderate success in 1978. Had anything worthwhile been written in the two decades since?

In the chapters that follow, I share some of these columns; you may judge for yourself.

Chapter Five

The Matter of Ethnicity

Ethnic stereotyping may not be of great concern to most Americans, but for those who have encountered it frequently, it is a troubling matter. "From the Frying Pan" addressed this issue from time to time. The story that follows, published in the *Pacific Citizen* on October 5, 1990, when the United States was preparing to fight Saddam Hussein's Iraqi troops in the Persian Gulf, effectively introduces the subject.

There is no way to tell how many of the quarter million Americans in the desert, aboard warships, and at air bases are Japanese Americans. By the law of averages, it is likely that some of them are, perhaps the sons and grandsons (and daughters and granddaughters, too) of Japanese Americans who served in World War II, Korea, and Vietnam.

I thought about that the other day while thumbing through the souvenir booklet published for the National AJA Veterans Reunion in Hawaii early last summer. It contains a reprint of a piece called "Poston Samurai" by Vince Tajiri, which was written in 1988 on the occasion of a salute to Japanese American vets of the Vietnam war and Vincent Okamoto, one of that war's genuine heroes.

Tajiri wrote that Okamoto was asked to counsel the son of a Nisei 442nd vet who was having a rough time overcoming his experience in Vietnam. What Okamoto heard from the Vietnam vet was chilling.

This young soldier was hit three times in battle, one of the wounds shattering his jaw. Let Tajiri go on with the story.

"The medics patch him up and, looking for other wounds, strip his clothes off. In bandaging the jaw, they have to work vertically—like a guy with a toothache—so now he's down to his shorts and he can't utter a sound. They load him and a wounded black buddy on a chopper to take them to the evac hospital. Just as they're about to take off, they load on three wounded North Vietnamese. The officer in charge tells the crew chief, 'Take these guys back for interrogation.'

"As they take off, they get heavy rifle fire. The chopper is overloaded, so the pilot yells to the crew chief to get rid of the gooks. The crew chief shoves each of the NVA guys out of the opening and then grabs the kid (the Japanese American), who is in a morphine daze and can't talk because of the bandages around his chin, and pulls him towards the door. By now they're more than 300 feet off the ground. The kid grabs the crew chief and won't let go. Just then, the black looks over, sees what's happening, and shouts, 'Hey, that guy's an American!' The crew chief apologizes and pulls him away from the door.

"It doesn't end there. When they get to the hospital, the Japanese American, naked and unable to talk, finds that he mistakenly is placed in a tent with the enemy's wounded. During the long, restless night when he slips in and out of consciousness, he hears a nurse complaining about having to tend to gooks who've been killing 'our boys.' The doctor replies, 'Yeah, I'd just as soon kill all these slants.' "

If there is any consolation, it's that Japanese Americans this time aren't likely to be mistaken for Iraqis by their stereotypically blind fellow Yanks.

But I, too, found myself guilty of stereotyping—and was chagrined by the realization—as the following column, published on October 4, 1991, relates.

The barber in my neighborhood is Chris Montoya, and as the name indicates, he is of Hispanic descent. Chris and his wife run a combination barbershop-beauty parlor in a shopette not far from my home, and they do a pretty darned good business.

But this is not a column about barbers or barbershops, but about what happened one recent day when I had dropped in to, as we used to say, have my ears lowered.

While I was waiting my turn, a couple came in with a teenage lad, presumably their son, who obviously needed a haircut. All three, by their appearance, were Hispanics, and apparently they spoke no English.

There are very few Hispanic customers who show up at Chris's place because it's not in the right neighborhood for that kind of clientele, but he took in the situation quickly. He spoke to the three in Spanish. There was an animated conversation back and forth for a short while, and then the teenager was escorted to a chair and another barber took over while his parents seated themselves.

Later, as he began to snip away at my hair, Chris said something like this: "I don't get much opportunity to talk Spanish anymore. I had to think about the words and do a little mental gear-shifting when I talked to those customers."

I asked Chris whether he spoke Spanish at home.

"No," he said, "my wife and I and the kids all speak English. I didn't even speak much Spanish when I was growing up down in the Valley. I know Spanish, but if you don't have any occasion to use it, you forget."

Chris's problem with Spanish isn't much different from the problem that Nisei and some Sansei experience with Japanese. They know something about the ancestral tongue, usually enough to make themselves understood if there is a need. But the need does not arise very often, so the tongue becomes rusty with disuse. And that's too bad.

But in appearance, Chris is a Hispanic, just as Japanese Americans look Asian. People have a tough time ridding themselves of stereotypes, and they expect anyone who looks Hispanic to be fluent in Spanish, just as they expect Japanese Americans to be fluent in Japanese.

I suppose I was guilty of stereotyping when I asked Chris about the language he uses at home. Why should it be anything other than English even though he looks Hispanic? Why should anyone look at me and ask whether we speak Japanese at home?

We don't, but they still ask questions. Just the way I did.

Some years later, I discovered to my chagrin that I was still making stereotypical judgments. In penance I wrote the following column on November 21, 1997.

If I were to ask my friend the Reverend Nobuko Miyake-Stoner, she no doubt would tell me confession is good for the soul. Since I know that my soul needs all the help it can get, let me make a confession.

One day not long ago, on a physician's instructions, I made an appointment at a pulmonary laboratory in a local hospital. It seems he had some concerns about how well my breathing system was functioning. As many may know, a pulmonary lab is a place where technicians have you suck in as much air as you can and then blow it out, fill your lungs and empty them, and perform other such tricks to see what kind of curves your ventilating system can produce on a computer screen. I did not know this when I checked in at the lab, but that is neither here nor there.

Apparently business was slow, and all the technicians were in a side room enjoying a coffee break or something. A trim young Caucasian woman in one of those white laboratory coats, looking very efficient, came out to ask my business. I showed her the documents that I had been told to bring.

She checked them briefly and then said, "Okay, we'll get started in a minute."

At that moment, some man in the side room said something like, "Do you want me to take this one?"

I traced the voice to a large black man. Almost immediately I remembered newspaper stories about minority students getting special treatment in medical schools under "equal opportunity" regulations, being accepted for classes even though their grades weren't high enough, and being graduated even though they weren't really qualified. The question that came to my mind was, was he really qualified? Or was he one of those who had slipped into the system?

These were unfair doubts. I had never met the man, never talked to him, never even seen him except at a distance. I knew nothing about his training or experience, but suddenly I found myself hoping I wouldn't become his patient.

I needn't have been concerned. The young woman said something like, "No, I can take care of it," and led me into the laboratory. It was obvious she knew her business, and I was pleased she was working with me.

While the tests were under way, the black man came into the laboratory and sat down at a desk and began to shuffle some papers. There was small talk between him and the white technician, and then something became very clear: the black man was the boss, the departmental supervisor, and the white woman was one of his assistants. Although she was very competent, the black man probably knew more about the tests being administered than she did.

There should have been no question about his qualifications, but I had been guilty of an unfair snap judgment about a person's competence based solely on skin color, the sort of thing I had been fighting for as long as I can remember.

Perhaps I should have apologized to him. But at the moment, I didn't have the courage.

So I have made my confession, and now I hope I will feel better about it tomorrow. P.S.—The tests turned out OK.

Part of the problem of identity, in addition to appearance, is that Japanese Americans identify themselves as Japanese Americans rather than simply as Americans. I touched on the matter in a column published on October 14, 1983.

If you met a tall, sandy-haired, blue-eyed American for the first time, would you go out of your way to ask him whether he was from Norway or Germany? Not likely. We simply assume he's American, and ethnic background doesn't come up very often in casual conversation unless it's directly pertinent to what's being talked about.

The answer to such a question may be something like this: "Well, I guess there's some Norwegian and German in me, plus some English and Irish and maybe some Dutch and Polish, but that goes back a long, long way, and I'm not sure what my background is. I guess I'm mostly American."

But Americans think nothing of asking fellow Americans of Asian descent whether they are from China or Japan. Most times the question seems to be asked out of innocent curiosity, but what irritates many Asian Americans is the implication that they are Asian rather than American.

A recent communication from Motoko Yasuda Lee, an associate professor of sociology at Iowa State University gets into this matter, and I'd like to share some of her thinking. She writes:

"I am an American of Japanese descent. I happen to be an Issei (born in Japan and naturalized) married to a man born and reared in China. I do not introduce myself as a Japanese American. My argument is this: unless others are saying, 'I am an English American' or 'I am a French American,' why should we keep saying 'I am a Japanese American'?

"I am very proud of my native land, and have no intention of hiding my ancestry. However, by attaching a modifier in front of a noun, minorities will remain minorities forever.

"I found similar symptoms among professional groups. I resent people calling me a female faculty member, or a minority faculty member, when they call others just faculty members. Thus, my practice has been to say, 'I am an American of Japanese descent or just an American.'

"We have to educate not only the 'majority,' but also minorities themselves in order to have them abandon the minority/majority mentality. . . . We ourselves have to start shaking off this minority mentality and insisting on equal treatment in all situations."

Right on.

Mrs. Lee's husband, whose first name she doesn't mention, has a clever way of putting things in perspective. When someone asks him what country he's from, he replies: "Originally from China. How about yourself?"

Some Nisei and Sansei reply to that kind of question: "My parents (or grandparents, or great-grandparents) were immigrants from Japan. How about you?"

A nice gentle put-down that has the advantage of provoking thought.

Total racial integration in America is an ideal that has yet to be realized. And it may never come to pass because of the disparate cultures we bring to the national table. This isn't altogether bad; American culture can be enriched by the amalgamation of many different heritages. But sometimes the effort to create a one-size-fits-all society can lead to situations that need to be handled lightheartedly, as this column published on August 17, 1984, points out:

A few weeks ago, a certain well-known chain store sent me a colorful flyer advertising goblets to be etched with one's own family coat of arms. The idea was that if you applied, their experts in heraldry would locate your coat of arms, etch it into a crystal goblet, and give it to you at no cost other than handling charges. The gimmick was that you would become so enthralled by the prospect of owning a whole set of similarly engraved goblets that you would buy them, one a month, for what seemed to be a remarkably high price.

How I got on their mailing list, I do not know. How they expected to find a coat of arms for a family named Hosokawa, I know not either. But a prank began to take shape. I filled out the application form, carefully printing the letters of my name into the blanks provided, and sent it off to see what would happen.

In time a letter, but no free goblet, arrived. I quote:

"Recently, you responded to an offer to research the Hosokawa Family Coat-of-Arms which was borne in the past by a family with the same name as the one you requested. We have looked through the thousands of Coats-of-Arms we already have on file, and we have looked through the many heraldic volumes in our library. Also, we have checked names from which yours may have been derived, but without success.

"We do not 'invent' a Coat-of-Arms where we cannot establish that one actually existed for a family name. Therefore, we will be unable to fill your order for Coat-of-Arms crystal. Naturally, there will be no charge for research."

Well, darn, foiled again. Nine or ten years ago, I received a somewhat similar letter offering me a "Hosokawa Coat of Arms" in full color for only $19.95. I wish I had accepted the offer just to see what they would send me. But at the time I did not have $19.95 to invest, and I lost the opportunity to see what was described as "an exclusive and particularly beautiful Coat of Arms" of a Japanese family as recreated by an American artist.

If we were to be completely honest about it, a Hosokawa coat of arms would not include lions and dragons and could not include knights in armor and helmets and lances. As I envisioned it when the offer first came up, stalks of rice would be more appropriate, perhaps rampant on a rice paddy under crossed chopsticks. Growing food, and getting enough to eat, were a lot more important to my peasant ancestors than riding into glorious combat.

But like most Japanese families, we do have a *mon,* or family crest. It appears in books, and I found it chiseled into the headstone of Grandfather Hosokawa's grave in a quiet bamboo grove on a hill above the humble house where he lived and died.

The *mon* looks vaguely like the dial on an old-fashioned telephone, with eight round "stars" encircling a larger round "star." What it all stands for, I am not certain. But I found a tie clip bearing this *mon* on sale at the tobacco and news stand at the Imperial Hotel in Tokyo, and now I wear it proudly.

The *mon* is genuine, and a coat of arms would not be for me. We're pleased that the mail-order folks are not going to "invent" something phony.

Even after a century or so, some Americans fail to understand that one doesn't have to be white—or black, for that matter—to be a citizen.

It still irritates some Japanese Americans to be considered foreign, or, at least, not quite American, by well-meaning but ignorant persons, and this subject was addressed periodically in "From the Frying Pan." The following column appeared on December 13, 1985.

There's nothing that irks a Japanese American more than to be told by someone with a white face that he speaks English well. Why shouldn't he? It's his first language. He was born in the U.S., educated in American schools, and possibly has never been out of the country except for brief trips as a tourist or perhaps as a member of the U.S. armed forces. If he (or she) didn't speak English well, there'd be something wrong.

Of course, the dolt who makes the comment means it as a compliment. But by that action he demonstrates his ignorance. He fails to understand that people with Asian faces also can be native-born Americans. He assumes, out of thoughtlessness or ignorance or unintended racism, that one must be white to be able to speak English. He needs to be corrected and educated. He needs to be put down so devastatingly that he'll never forget the lesson.

Most of us can't think of the properly devastating thing to say at the moment of the affront. So our retort lacks the proper sting. We say something accurate but inadequate, like: "Of course I speak English, I was born in the United States."

Compare that to the remark attributed to Wellington Koo, a Western-educated Chinese diplomat. According to the story, he was at a luncheon when a fellow at the table, attempting to be friendly, asked:

"You likee soupie?"

Koo smiled, nodded, and continued with his lunch.

A short while later, Koo was introduced as the luncheon speaker. He rose and delivered his speech in magnificent English. Then, as he sat down, he turned to the man at his table and asked quietly, "You likee speechie?"

Congressman Norman Mineta of California is credited with a more Americanized put-down. It happened at the dedication of the Fremont plant in California where General Motors and

Toyota are now building cars in a joint venture. Mineta was called on to say a few words, which he delivered with his usual vigor and polish. This impressed a high GM official to the point that he was moved to compliment the Nisei congressman on his ability to speak English.

Mineta's completely American appropriate retort: "Thanks. You might be interested to know I'm familiar with two more words. (Expletive) you!"

A more gentle response, which I heard recently, goes like this: "Thank you very much. You speak English very well, too. Where did you learn it?"

The column then invited its readers to submit suggestions for the most devastating put-down. The response, which included an admonishing letter from Gordon Hamachi of Oakland, California, led to a second column on January 31, 1986. Hamachi asked:

"Do you really advocate responding with a devastating put-down when someone ignorantly and inadvertently offends you? What you proposed to do is worse than what is done to you; your offender has no idea that what he does is wrong, while you act with a deliberate intent to hurt him. This is simple revenge which will not correct or educate; it will only foster rage, humiliation, and more bad feelings toward all Asian Americans. If you must have a contest, a far more constructive approach is to ask readers to send in accounts of the most amazing, bizarre and ridiculous incidents that you have experienced. By making these stories known you can give your readers an awareness of the problem and its ramifications."

As a matter of fact, various entries did relate amazing incidents. In the column, I wrote:

I like Philadelphian Judge Bill Marutani's erudite answer to someone who compliments him with, "My, but you speak English good." Marutani's response: "No, sir. You speak English good; I speak it well."

Esther Torii Suzuki of St. Paul recalls that when she went to Minnesota to attend college during the war, a stranger asked directions, complimented her English, and asked how long she had been here. "Two weeks," Esther replied. When the stranger expressed amazement that anyone could speak English so well after only two weeks, Esther responded: "I'm a linguistic genius."

Naomi Kashiwabara of San Diego says when someone complimented his English, he replied, "Thank you, I couldn't speak a word when I came to this country." Next question: "When was that?" Kashiwabara's response: "I was born here."

The winner was a puckish entry likely to leave the target scratching his head and wondering what's going on. George Wakiji of Alexandria, Virginia, who, after being asked where he learned to speak English so well, responds:

"I studied English at U-C-R-A. As you can tell, I still have difficulty with my L's."

Let me tell you some true stories about certain Americans who failed to understand that ethnic Asians can be Americans—and should have known better. In July 1981, a state dinner was held at the White House to honor Japanese prime minister Zenko Suzuki. Among the guests was Spark Matsunaga, a decorated American war hero and junior senator from the state of Hawaii. Just before President Ronald Reagan's arrival and the start of the dinner, the Japanese and American guests were escorted to separate waiting rooms. Senator and Mrs. Matsunaga found themselves being herded into the Japanese room. Secretary of State Alexander Haig also was in the Japanese room, and like a good host he went around introducing himself to Suzuki's aides. As the *Washington Post* reported, he then

approached Matsunaga to welcome him to the United States. A bemused Matsunaga put on his best dime-store Japanese accent and told Haig that it had been his pleasure to vote for his confirmation in the Senate.

"You should have seen his face," said Matsunaga.

An obviously flustered Haig still did not recognize Matsunaga.

It took a helpful Japanese visitor to identify the senator for the secretary of state.

On another occasion, Congressman Mineta learned he had not been invited to a White House dinner for Japanese prime minister Masayoshi Ohira. When someone on his staff inquired about the omission, there were red-faced apologies and the explanation that the White House people who drew up the guest list thought Mineta was of Italian ancestry. An invitation was delivered belatedly, and Mineta ignored it, explaining later that he thought Prime Minister Ohira was Irish.

Not even a senator as distinguished as Daniel Inouye of Hawaii was immune. Inouye, a member of the Senate committee looking into the Watergate scandal, was insulted on national television during the hearings in the summer of 1973, and that led to the following column on August 10:

If the sorry drama of the Watergate hearings had drifted off into a distant and dreary realm of late for Japanese American television viewers, it came back with a jolt last week when John J. Wilson, attorney for deposed White House aides H. R. Haldeman and John D. Ehrlichman, angrily referred to Senator Daniel K. Inouye as "that little Jap."

There was Wilson on national television in living color, face livid, hotly repeating a statement made earlier to a newspaperman. It was no unwitting slip of the tongue, no casual reference; it was only too obviously a racial slur flung out with calculated rancor. The questions of the television reporters crowded around Wilson with microphones reflected the shock that reverberated around the country. . . .

At times some of us have considered the Japanese American Citizens League's campaign against the use of "Jap" excessively touchy, for there is a need to distinguish between innocent usage and its use as a hate word. Wilson left no doubt and his explanation—"I consider it a description of the man. I wouldn't mind being called a little American"—was lame. Would he have called Senator Joseph Montoya, another member of the Watergate committee, a little Spic?

The vagaries of language usage can be confusing. For example, it is proper to call a section of a city "Chinatown," but it is offensive to call males who live there "Chinamen." People from Sweden are Swedes, people from Turkey are Turks, and people of the Jewish faith are Jews. That's all quite proper. But to call a Japanese a "Jap" is to invite violence. "Jap" is offensive because historically it was a term of hate and derision, and it evokes bitter memories even when employed innocently, which is most often the case today. Not many years ago, African Americans hated to be called black. Now many regard the term as proper and wear it as a badge of pride. There seems to be a lot of maturity in refusing to be upset by a word that is not used maliciously.

From time to time, my column chided Japanese Americans for being excessively sensitive about the term "Jap," asserting that in most instances it was used innocently and that it would be wiser not to be uptight about it. On April 5, 1985, I wrote:

Late last month Denver hosted one of the regional semifinals of the NCAA basketball tournament, and our local sports pages were in their glory. For the record, let it be noted that St. John's defeated Kentucky, and North Carolina State defeated Alabama. Then St. John's defeated North Carolina State 69–60 and won the right to go to Lexington, Kentucky, to play for the national championship.

North Carolina State's coach is Jim Valvano. St. John's is coached by Lou Carnesecca. Both are of Italian origin and proud of it. They talk about how much they love Italian food and revel in the sweeping stereotypical gestures we've come to associate with Italians. The local press picked up on it and made a big thing of the Italian-ness.

Was anybody offended? No, they loved it.

Did anybody think Valvano and Carnesecca were Italians rather than Americans? Of course not. Valvano and Carnesecca were just a couple of darned good American basketball coaches who happened to have Italian backgrounds and wasn't it an interesting coincidence?

Well, now, let's take a hypothetical but somewhat parallel situation.

Let's say the two coaches who took their basketball teams to the semifinals of a stirring national tournament were Japanese Americans named Jim Yamada and Lou Suzuki. That's not too far-fetched; there are some darned good Nisei and Sansei basketball coaches making a name for themselves. And now for some questions raised by their presence:

Would the press make a thing of their Japanese-ness the way it did about the Italian-ness of Valvano and Carnesecca? If so, why? If not, why not?

Would it be because Italians are supposed to be jolly and lovable, while the Japanese stereotypically are too serious and too earnest and not the kind to have fun with? Would it be because Italy as a nation poses no economic threat to the United States? Would it be because Italians are members of the American racial majority and Japanese aren't and therefore must be treated with a little more sensitivity? Or treated with less sensitivity?

If the press noted that Yamada and Suzuki were of Japanese descent, should we consider that racist and offensive because their ancestry isn't pertinent to their abilities as basketball coaches?

If the press failed to note that Yamada and Suzuki were of Japanese descent, should we consider that offensive (as some did when they thought Sansei astronaut Ellison Onizuka wasn't properly recognized) because credit isn't going where credit is due?

And finally, is this a matter that we ought to be concerning ourselves about? If so, why? And if not, why not?

I don't pretend to have answers to questions like these. But I do think they are pertinent in searching for what some of the deep and earnest thinkers in our midst refer to as our "identities."

I returned to the subject in a column published on February 23, 1990, which said, in part:

You may have noticed a commercial on TV recently that has to do with using your hands to speak Italian. The guy is selling frozen pizzas or spaghetti sauce or something like that, I don't recall for sure, and he says the way to speak Italian is to wave your hands and shrug your shoulders and use certain words that I cannot remember at the moment.

One way to look at the commercial is to say it is the most demeaning kind of stereotyping, which I think it is. But if there have been protests, they've escaped me. Perhaps most people don't think the commercial stereotypes Italians, and so they think nothing of it. Mario Cuomo doesn't talk like that, and neither does Lee Iacocca. Everybody knows it, so why fuss about a silly TV commercial?

Now let's look at this from another angle. Suppose, instead of a television commercial mimicking a stereotypical Italian, someone was mimicking a stereotypical Japanese, hissing through his teeth and bobbing his head and grinning toothy grins and saying "Ah, so" while peddling soy sauce or instant noodles.

Some questions: How would you as a Japanese American feel about the Japanese stereotype? What would you do about it, and why?

Perception can be an unfunny matter depending on the eye, or the ear, of the beholder. Some time ago I learned that in Boston it's a no-no to refer to police vehicles as paddy wagons. Why? Because for some folks it brings back memories of days when male Irish immigrants, often referred to as Paddy, were being picked up frequently for public drunkenness.

Tread softly in these sensitive times. "Newspaperman" is no longer proper, since women tell us they also are journalists as well as chairpersons. Fortunately, we all continue to be humans.

The sad thing about all this is that many stereotypes used today are not meant to hurt. But some hurt more than others. On March 11, 1988, I wrote:

We walked into a restaurant one recent day, and there on the wall next to the table was a caricature figure of the traditional Irishman. Wide grin in a homely square face. Red beard. Cane in hand and a tall green hat atop the head. Obviously it was designed to promote the St. Patrick's Day spirit, whatever that might mean, and perhaps get customers in the mood to buy more drinks.

"Cute little figure," one might say, and smile. On St. Pat's day everyone is an Irishman, and no one takes offense at the stereotype of the happy, drunken, amusing son of the Ould Sod.

Ah, but wait a minute. What if the caricature figure were a Hispanic with drooping mustache and wide sombrero in anticipation of Cinco de Mayo, or a black with a huge wedge of watermelon to advertise fresh fruit on the menu. Or, horrors, a buck-toothed and bespectacled Japanese with camera hanging from his neck pitching some product or another. Would we be similarly amused? Not likely.

Fortunately, the more offensive of racial stereotypes have pretty well vanished due in large part to the strenuous protests of those offended. Yet it is a curious thing that some stereotypes are completely acceptable, and others are painfully offensive. What makes each of them that way?

I got to thinking about this again the other night after seeing *Crocodile Dundee* on the telly. Paul Hogan plays the part of the unsophisticated outdoorsman from the Australian bush who gains fame for having slain a crocodile that was about to devour him. A fetching New York reporter comes to interview him, witnesses a rousing fistfight in a fly-specked frontier bar just like in our Westerns, and lures him to the effete New York scene. An entertaining picture, but nothing to send you away worried about the future of the world.

By coincidence, the next day there was a story in the morning paper about Australians who fear *Crocodile Dundee* gives the world a false impression of their country being peopled by beer-swilling louts. Australians, their spokesmen say, are really quite cultured and sophisticated.

I don't recall Americans ever protesting that their movies and television programs that feature wildly exaggerated Western barroom brawls and gunfights, renegade bushwhackers, and Indian-killers gave folks the wrong impression about their antecedents. In fact we don't bother to think that the stereotypes are harmful, or else we take a kind of perverse pride in the bad-man reputation.

What it boils down to, I guess, is that most stereotypes, while they contain elements of painful truth, won't harm you if you don't let them bother you. The Irish have such a reputation for boisterous drinking that it's hard to live up to it, and rather than be outraged by the stereotype, my Irish friends seem to enjoy the friendly notoriety.

Of course there's a vast gulf between friendly stereotypes and hostile ones, but I would guess even the friendliest ones were malicious in the beginning. When the targeted simply refused to get mad, there wasn't much fun in ridiculing them. We might want to think about that.

The interesting difference between the Chinese American and Japanese American approach to ethnic background was discussed in a column published on November 16, 1984.

About a month ago, Vice President George Bush visited San Francisco's Chinatown in a search for votes. We were in the middle of a presidential election campaign, remember? I happened to see the extensive coverage given the event by *Asian Week,* a San Francisco newspaper that calls itself "An English Language Journal for the Asian American Community."

"Bush was greeted by extended applause and prancing lion dancers as his limousine pulled up in front of the Supreme Pastry shop on Stockton Street," *Asian Week* reported. "He walked to the corner of Jackson Street and then started working his way up the clogged sidewalks, shaking hands and kissing babies.

"He was handed a white butcher's smock and apron outside the Sang Sang Market and the Canton Market, where he stopped to carve a slice of roast pig and then roast duck, which he ate. . . .

"With merchants offering him Chinese food and souvenirs almost every step of the way, Bush then turned down Jackson Street and made his way to the Grand Palace on Grant Avenue.

A small group of about 30 prominent community leaders awaited him inside the restaurant. As the Vice President and his wife sat down to a table for some dim sum . . ."

Asian Week also published a number of photographs, some of which showed a long banner behind the head table. The banner carried three rows of Chinese characters, which I cannot read, and one line in English: "San Francisco Chinese Welcome Vice President and Mrs. Bush."

John T.C. Fang, publisher of *Asian Week,* spoke at the restaurant reception, saying that San Francisco's Chinese American community makes up 14 percent of the city's population, that some twenty Chinese-language newspapers are published there, and that a half-dozen Chinese-language schools are in the immediate vicinity of Chinatown. Fang was quoted in his newspaper: "The Chinese consider San Francisco Chinatown the capital city and the Chinese cultural center of America. But we are Americans also, and we are proud to welcome our vice president today."

Why all this attention in this column to a month-old political event in an election that is now history?

The point I want to make is that Chinese Americans proudly proclaim their Chinese ancestry and cultural background, while, broadly speaking, Japanese Americans with equal pride seem to be more inclined to emphasize their Americanism. Correct?

Had George Bush strolled through Li'l Tokyo in Los Angeles, would he have been invited to slice himself a piece of sashimi or cook himself a shrimp tempura? Would the welcome banner over the head table have carried three lines of Japanese characters and one line of English? Would the speaker have told Bush about the number of Japanese-language schools and newspapers in the community? Or would the emphasis have been on the way ethnic Japanese have become part and parcel of the greater American community, taking leading roles in business, teaching in schools, being elected to public office?

This isn't the place to pass judgment as to which approach is "better," but only to point out the difference. And it would make an interesting study to determine why the difference exists.

Let me share one more "ethnic" column with you. It was published on July 7, 1995.

If you haven't heard of Pocahontas lately, you've been neglecting your newspaper reading and television watching. They have been busy, busy, busy telling us about the charm and moneymaking potential of the latest animated film, based on the Pocahontas story, produced by the entertainment wizards of the Disney organization.

Pocahontas, we have been reminded time and again, was an Indian princess living in what is now Virginia when some English settlers showed up in 1607. Taking possession of land that didn't belong to them, the settlers established Jamestown, the first permanent English settlement in North America.

As was so often the case, the Indians took a dim view of being invaded. Fighting broke out, and Pocahontas's father, Chief Powhatan, captured Captain John Smith. According to the story, Powhatan was about to execute Smith when Pocahontas bravely threw herself on Smith and persuaded her father to cease and desist.

Whether all this is true or not, it makes a touching story. The Disney folks are not reluctant to animate for projection in theaters and TV such various subjects as mice, witches, dwarf miners, puppets, fawns, lions, and tender young females like Snow White, Cinderella, and now Pocahontas.

The snippets of the Pocahontas film I've seen in TV promotionals show the Indian princess to be slim, doe-eyed, fetching, and somewhat dusky, while Captain Smith is large, muscular, handsome, and blond. Which brings up the point I wish to make in this column.

Does it seem to you, as it does to me, that almost invariably in literature and song it is the Caucasian male who crosses the color line and wins the non-Caucasian female's heart?

Why isn't it the reverse—the Indian brave, the Moslem prince, the African chieftain or the Japanese samurai who woos and carries away the fair European? In the few films in which the dark guy gets the girl, it seems the guy kidnaps the woman, with heroic Caucasian males dashing to her rescue.

There are exceptions, of course. In the early days of film, Rudolph Valentino, of Italian origins, played the role of a desert sheik who fed the fantasies of American women. The King of Siam (alias Yul Brynner, with a haircut that would qualify him for the National Basketball Association) was allowed to charm Anna, the Englishwoman who was hired to educate his children. And don't forget Othello, Shakespeare's brave, powerful, dark-skinned Moslem general, and his beautiful wife, Desdemona.

But even in these exceptions, there often is tragedy rather than happiness ever after. Othello is successful in his profession and blissfully married but is wrongly convinced that Desdemona has been unfaithful, and he strangles her. (How long will it be before there is a Broadway play or operetta based on O.J. Simpson's travails?)

Let me share a movie idea with you for reversing the stereotype of the white man crossing racial barriers to win a nonwhite girl. There's this Japanese baseball pitcher, see, and despite a funny windup, he wins a lot of games and becomes the darling of the starlets in Los Angeles, where he works. One thing leads to another and—well, you get the idea, don't you?

Chapter Six

The Next Generation

Thirty-Five Years in the Frying Pan contained a number of columns about the four children Alice and I reared—their triumphs and tragedies and the business of coping with an unfamiliar world. These columns were popular with readers who were also raising young families. But in time, our children grew up and moved away. We were fortunate that they stayed out of trouble, fit easily into middle-class society, and did well professionally and economically. If they faced traumas like those of my youth, I was unaware of it. Times were changing.

Mike, my eldest son, became assistant dean for curriculum at the University of Missouri Medical School. The next in line, Susan Hosokawa Boatright, is a counselor and English teacher in the Denver Public Schools, where her husband is a mathematics teacher. Pete, the third child, is a nationally recognized guru in the electronic cash-transfer business, the details of which I find completely unfathomable. Christie Hosokawa Harveson, smart as a whip in her own quiet way, married an air force officer who became an airline pilot, and they raised three fine youngsters.

It was difficult to write anything about my adult offspring without embarrassing them, but when grandchildren began to arrive, I could write about them instead. The world they came into was altogether different from that of my childhood. For one thing, it was far more complex. For another, they seldom encountered the confusion and the prejudice that I—and even their bicultural parents, on occasion—experienced. My grandchildren were raised in typical American households, with virtually no trace of Japanese culture.

One of my regrets is that none of my issue, with the exception of Mike, had the opportunity to know my father. Although this chapter is about my grandchildren and their reaction to the strange world they inhabit, I would like to open with a column about my father, who left his native Japanese village in 1899, when he was a lad of fifteen, and crossed the ocean to seek his fortune in America.

If there is such a thing as a stereotypical Japanese, my father would have fit. He was short and stocky and had a bristling mustache. He wore glasses to correct severe myopia. He worked hard until late in life, when he decided it was more fun to take it easy. He did a pretty good job of mangling the English language.

What distinguished him from most of his contemporaries, who were inclined to be stoics, was that he was a marvelous raconteur. He could entertain his friends by the hour with stories about his experiences, about people he had known, about things he had seen. He made the fun of his boyhood in rural Japan a shared pleasure. He had his audiences roaring in laughter, even though they had heard the stories many times, about his misadventures as a young immigrant in the strange land called America.

He loved to tell about going fishing and the big ones that eluded him (although in reality he was an excellent fisherman), and going out to shoot pheasant and stuffing a cabbage into the pocket in the back of his jacket to make it look as though he were a more successful hunter than he was. He had a knack for making those stories come alive, and he enjoyed entertaining his friends with them.

In short, he had a sense of humor. He could be serious, but he knew how to laugh. He thought laughter was an important part of life, and he had a wonderful time helping others to laugh.

How many Nisei do you know with that kind of talent? Oh, sure, there are guys like Pat Morita, who makes a good living as a comedian, and the late Goro Suzuki of stage and television, who as Jack Soo could make people laugh simply by looking mournful. But they are the exceptions. Most of the rest of us are overly earnest and sober-sided, acting as if the weight of the world's ills and sorrows rests on our shoulders and it is our destiny, indeed our obligation, to wear sackcloth until we succeed in banishing them.

It can be argued that there isn't much to laugh about when you're preoccupied with the injustice of current racism and with redress for long-past wrongs, which we are told we should be doing. Of course these are pressing matters. But surely there must be more to life than anger, frustration, and outrage, and more involved in leadership than stirring up those moods.

I am grateful that my father, who like most Issei lived a life more harsh by far than that of Nisei and Sansei, taught me the pleasure of laughter. It would be a sorry thing to forget how to smile, at least once in a while.

I never knew my father-in-law. I regret that, because he must have been an interesting fellow. It is likely he could have told me some things about his daughter, who became my wife, that would have been useful. Be that as it may, on September 9, 1983, I was prompted to write about him after the arrival of a mysterious package.

I have not written of my father-in-law because I never knew him. He died at an early age some years before I met his daughter, who in time became my wife. His name was Taro Miyake, not to be mistaken with a professional wrestler of that name. The Taro Miyake of whom I write today was a wrestling fan, but he made his precarious living as editor and publisher of a small weekly Japanese-language newspaper in Portland, Oregon.

I have heard bits and pieces about Taro Miyake. He was a kind and gregarious man. When his wife sent him out to collect on some bills due him, chances were that he would sit down for a warm, happy conversation, and the matter of money never would come up. He loved to fish, and to eat.

But I write of him today for other reasons. The other day a small package came in the mail. It was a book of haiku poems by Miyake published in 1937. Some old friend of his had discovered it among her possessions, and she wanted Miyake's daughter to have it. There were other copies, of course, but they must have been lost during the war.

It is a shame that we cannot read and appreciate the poems. We have no idea what they are about. Do they tell of the beautiful Oregon that he had made his home? Are they about the land he left as a youth, the thoughts he had as he struggled to make a living and support his family? Does he speak in anger or philosophically about the discrimination that he faced as an Oriental in a white man's land?

He must have written about all these subjects, but we will not know until we find someone to read and translate the poems for us. What we do know from the fact that he wrote haiku and had them published was that he was a sensitive man, a cultured man. We had known earlier that he had been a prize-winning photographer. He experimented with tinting his art-quality prints, and some of them had been accepted for shows. Now his poems reveal another dimension.

As a group, the Issei displayed many talents. They could sing the classics, play the bamboo flute and other instruments, perform the kabuki, write critical essays and poems. Some were eloquent speakers. Others were painters and calligraphers.

Among the women were accomplished teachers of tea ceremony and flower arrangement, singers and dancers. Some, like Taro Miyake's wife, Tora, had been educated in mission schools and had learned the piano and other Western instruments.

In many respects, the Issei were a remarkable people. They worked with enormous energy and zeal, but they also knew that life needed cultural enrichment. And a little book, written by a relative I never had the opportunity to meet, reminded me of that fact.

Several chapters in the first Frying Pan book were devoted to the older grandchildren—Ashlyn and Michael Hosokawa, who are Mike's kids, and their cousin, Patrick Hosokawa, whose father is Pete. Ashlyn is now a hospital dietitian in Columbia, Missouri, working on her master's degree. Michael is an engineer who spends a lot of time on steel platforms in the Gulf of Mexico, where he supervises the pumping of oil from underwater wells to onshore refineries. Patrick is a programmer in Denver, skilled in teaching computers to perform. This allows him a lifestyle quite unlike those of his parents and grandparents. Good computer programmers—and Patrick is one—don't have to worry about employment. So when he completes a project, which may take six months or more, he quits his job and spends time reading or traveling or wandering around in the cool woods. And when he is ready to go back to work, invariably there is an assignment waiting for him. Ah, me.

But this chapter will focus on the early years of the other five grandchildren—Matt Harveson, a former all-American swimmer who wants to be a swimming coach, his brother Jon, an aspiring actor, their sister Tiffany, who was a star six-foot-tall high school basketball player before going off to college to study engineering, plus Steven Boatright, now a college sophomore and soccer luminary, and his sister Stephanie, about whom you will read later. In my column of August 16, 1985, I wrote:

The age of six may be too tender to own a pocketknife, but Steve would not agree. We, just the two of us, went to see a swimming meet the other day, and he was scarcely belted into the car when, smiling broadly, he pulled a knife out of his pocket and displayed it for me.

I had never seen it before. It was a handsome red Swiss Army knife with two blades.

"Hey, oh wow, where did you get that?" I asked in the exaggerated tone adults for some reason use when talking to little kids.

"My Dad bought it for me at the sporting goods store."

"Wow," I said. "That's neat. But aren't you too little to have a real knife?"

"Naw," Steve replied. "I'll be careful with it."

"I know you will," I said. "But never forget that a pocketknife can be dangerous. It's a tool to cut wood and things, and not to cut other people or—"

"Or yourself," he broke in.

I was pleased. Steve had been briefed adequately before being entrusted with what may be the first symbol of the transition from babyhood to boyhood.

Over the years, I've owned dozens of pocketknives, including Boy Scout knives that had a built-in can opener–screwdriver, an awl, and, if I remember correctly, a corkscrew, in addition to a long blade and a short one. If I did not lose them, they became dull and refused to keep an edge, or they rusted, or the blade snapped off and the knives just disappeared. But I treasured each of them, and I could understand Steve's delight at owning his first.

Two of Steve's cousins, Matt and Jon Harveson, were swimming in the meet. Matt has grown into a lean, muscular thirteen-year-old who swims like a seal. Jon is a couple of years younger, and it is obvious that at his current stage of development, his chief talents lie in areas other than the pool, but he gives swimming a good try.

Each was entered in three or four or maybe five events, if you include the relay. Matt's big race was the 100-meter freestyle, in which he faced formidable competition. He was trailing after the first lap, but he made a good turn, and, stroking powerfully, he gained the lead. At the end he was pulling away and won handily. Jon did well too, placing in each of his races, although not in as spectacular a fashion as his brother.

The meet dragged on, and Steve and I had to leave before it was over. We missed the relay events entirely, but we know Matt and Jon had swum some good races. They will continue to practice, and before the summer is over their form and strength will improve and they will win many more races.

Steve is taking swimming lessons, too. It is too early to know whether he will be good enough to compete, but that really doesn't matter. The important thing is that he enjoy the water. He was quiet as we drove home, thinking, perhaps, of swimming but more likely fingering with pleasure the red knife in his pocket. The grandchildren are growing up, and in their experiences I see a repetition of the childhood pleasure my own youngsters enjoyed. And sometimes, as when I first saw Steve's knife, I recall my own boyhood so long, long ago.

Not much later, I was pressed into baby-sitting duty, a duty of grandfathers since time immemorial, and that experience resulted in the following column on August 8, 1986.

My grandson Steve, who is seven years old and an avid student of karate, has been asking for some time to see *Karate Kid, Part 2*. The other afternoon, we visited the neighborhood movie palace to fulfill his wish. To give his parents the full benefit of the free baby-sitter service, we took along Steve's little sister Stephanie, who at age three has only minimal interest in movies and even less interest in karate. The prospects for the outing, to put it optimistically, were not promising.

The day's first shock was the discovery that even in midafternoon of a weekday, the price of admission for all kids, regardless of size is $3. Oh, well. If Pat Morita gets a chunk of the ticket price—and I hope he does—it's money well spent. He can say as much as anyone in the acting business simply by raising an eyebrow, frowning, or being inscrutable, and in comparison to some other Hollywood types, I would say he deserves much more than what he is paid, whatever that is.

But to get back to the business at hand. These days it is necessary to eat popcorn while watching a movie. I do not know where or how the custom began, but it seems to be firmly entrenched, and the grandkids suggested it should be observed. A small box for the children amounted to $.75 apiece, plus tax. [In 1997, when I went to a movie again, a small sack of popcorn was $2.25.] They preferred individual servings over sharing.

Steve ate his popcorn at a judicious pace. Stephanie raced through hers at such a rapid rate that she had emptied the box even before Mr. Miyagi (Pat Morita) and his friend Daniel started for his home town in Okinawa.

The next offscreen episode should be predictable. "I'm thirsty," Stephanie proclaimed in a piping little soprano voice that somehow can be heard in the far corners of a movie theater. "Grandpa, I want something to drink. Right now."

To silence her, I promised 'some pop if she would be quiet for a little while. She was. For a little while.

Just as Mr. Miyagi was explaining to Daniel why Sato's gangsters were being so mean to them, Stephanie and I departed for the lobby to invest in some potables. Steve was so engrossed in the movie, the popcorn, and now the beverage, that it did not seem appropriate to ask him to fill me in on why the gangsters were so mean. I had to guess for the rest of the film.

The drink quenched Stephanie's thirst but only increased her restlessness. As gently as I could, I suggested she take a nap.

"I don't want to take a nap," she said in a voice now familiar to everyone in the theater. What she decided to do was crawl around in the aisle, exploring people's shoes and empty popcorn boxes and soft drink cups discarded by earlier patrons. Fortunately, Stephanie did not become thirsty again. Maybe the typhoon scene had something to do with it.

Presently, Steve and I saw the final sequence, when Daniel, desperately close to being killed, by a superhuman effort honks the villain's nose. End of *Karate Kid, Part 2.*

Stephanie will be somewhat older when she goes with Steve and me to see *Karate Kid, Part 3,* if and when it is produced. That's fine. But what worries me is that I, too, will be older and less able to cope with the strain of baby-sitting.

Steve's interest in karate led to something undoubtedly more useful in the long run. The matter was addressed in a column published April 3, 1987.

Our firstborn, Mike, was a toddler when Grandma lived with us. Since she was an Issei, she spoke Japanese. And since Mike spent a lot of time with her, he learned to speak Japanese. In fact, he learned to speak it quite well.

Alice and I speak English almost exclusively. Although both of us understood enough Japanese to carry on a conversation, having learned it from our parents in childhood, it was just more natural to speak in our native tongue, except in talking to Grandma.

But somehow little Mike got the impression that his parents didn't understand Japanese. So he took on the role of interpreter. When Grandma said something in Japanese, he'd tell us in English what she was saying. And when Alice or I said something in English, he'd translate it into Japanese for Grandma even though we might not have been talking to her. He did a pretty good job of it.

Unfortunately, Grandma had to leave us. After she was gone, Mike didn't hear Japanese anymore. And his parents, not being smart enough to know better, made no effort to let him hear Japanese being spoken, nor did they encourage him to continue using the language.

That was a long time ago. Mike still remembers a few words, but not many. And that's a pity, because Grandma had made a good start toward teaching him a second language.

Mike's little sister, Susan, was too young to come under Grandma's linguistic influence. So she was no better prepared to learn Japanese in Dr. Willie Nagai's class at the University of Colorado than her blonde and blue-eyed classmates.

Sad to relate, her efforts were less than successful. She hasn't retained much more of that experience than *Watakushi wa Nihongo ga wakarimasen,* which, as any first-year student knows, means "I do not understand Japanese."

But an interesting thing happened. Susan's son Steve, my grandson, has taken a lively interest in the ancestral language. He acquired the interest in his karate class, taught by a Caucasian who requires the students to learn to count to 100 in Japanese and to recognize a number of Japanese characters as well as karate technique.

The students learn the meaning of the characters, but not necessarily the sound. Take, for example, the character for "sun" which also is "day," which is pronounced *hi* or *nichi.* When that character is displayed, the kids recognize it as meaning either sun or day. But Steve is interested in even more. He wants to be able to speak the language.

Steve's parents, being wiser than his grandparents, have recognized his interest and are encouraging it. They have asked me to help him, and I have agreed happily. When we get together, we practice such useful phrases as *Onaka ga sukimashita* (I'm hungry), *Gakko wa omoshiroi desu ka?* (Is school fun?), and *Iie, gakko wa omoshiroku nai desu* (No, school is not fun).

Steve's accent is remarkably good. I have hope that I can do a better job of teaching my grandson than I did with my own offspring. Not many are given a second chance, and I do not want to flub it again.

Unfortunately, as Steve became busier and busier with school and soccer and hanging out, the Japanese lessons tapered off. But his interest was revived when he got to college. Conversational Japanese was one of the subjects he signed up for, and when memories of his earlier training returned, he did very well in class. Steve doesn't look Japanese, the result of his mixed parentage, so his instructor was surprised that he was such a good student. But one day Steve had to confess why he had an advantage over the others in the class.

Steve's sister, Stephanie, seems to share his facility with the language. When we visited Japan several years ago, she quickly learned the phrase *Ote-arai wa doko deska?* It means "Where is the bathroom?"

For a time, grandson Jon also showed an interest in learning Japanese and asked me to help. I made a tape of some common Japanese expressions and gave it to him, but I forgot about them when it appeared Jon's interest was fleeting. As it turned out, he had paid them some attention. After he graduated from the University of New Mexico, he joined an Up With People troupe comprised of young men and women from many countries who traveled around staging programs that featured happy songs and performing community service on the side. In his group were some young ladies from Japan who were curious about Jon's somewhat Japanese appearance. He proudly told them he was half Japanese, reached back into his memory for the phrases he had learned from my tapes, and proceeded to dazzle them with his language skills. "Happy New Year," he exclaimed, although it was midsummer. "This is a dog. What day is today? My name is Jon. What is your name? I like to eat noodles."

My grandson Matt, the swimmer, was no whiz at languages, but he did grow into a 200-pound man more than six feet tall. Some years before he achieved those proportions, he and I (somewhat reluctantly) engaged in a contest of strength that resulted in the following column published on April 17, 1987.

My father was not a large man. Heredity, combined with less than adequate nutrition in his youth, must have had something to do with it. (You ought to see the size of some of the younger Japanese today. Big-boned guys who stand six foot-plus are no rarity on the Ginza. Same heredity, different diet.)

But he had worked on the railroad in his youth and had done a lot of other hard physical labor. He had muscles. He and I used to have arm wrestling matches as I was growing up. For a long time, he could win without much effort.

Then one day I beat him. We tried again, and once more I won. We laughed, and I relished a sense of triumph. But I also felt a bit sad because I had defeated someone I looked up to.

In many families, arm wrestling between father and son is a kind of rite to measure the progress of the new generation against the, shall we say, decline of the older. It is a time of rejoicing when at last the son prevails, for it marks his approaching maturity.

I bring up all this because the other day I was egged into an arm wrestling match with Matt, my grandson, who at fourteen is a tall, well-muscled athlete. Also at fourteen he is still a boy and finds it difficult to refrain from exercising his superiority by poking and otherwise irritating his younger siblings.

Now, the simple way to put him in his place by showing he really wasn't so hot would have been to arrange an arm wrestling match between Matt and his father. But that would not be quite fair, since Matt's father is a large and powerful man. It will be years before Matt can hope to match his father's muscle.

Thus, someone came up with the idea that if Matt were to be defeated at arm wrestling by his frail, doddering, and semi-senile grandfather, he would be shamed into behaving. So I was set up. I wasn't certain until later what this was all about. I was simply told that it was very important that I should win.

Well, we put our elbows on the table and clasped hands, and on signal we began to strain. I locked my shoulder muscles and pulled, but Matt wouldn't give. Neither could he budge me. Meanwhile, all the siblings and parents and relatives were screaming and hollering for the underdog—me—to win.

It was like a high school wrestling match. Sweat broke out on my forehead. Matt grunted and strained. I grunted back and strained even harder, wondering if my heart would hold out.

In the end, age and endurance won. Matt weakened, and I pinned his arm. If there had been room in the kitchen, I would have been hoisted on shoulders and paraded around the table, for I had vanquished the young upstart. Matt, I'm proud to say, took defeat like a good sport, although he contended he was laughing so hard he couldn't use all his strength.

Soon Matt will demand a rematch, and I will have to give it to him out of sportsmanship. But I have no confidence that I will win again. He grows stronger by the day, and I, unfortunately, older by the hour. I just hope that by then he will have learned to be gracious and merciful in victory.

One of my older grandsons, Patrick, grew up away from Colorado, and I did not get to know him as well as some of the others. But he came back to attend the University of Colorado. On January 29, 1993, he was the subject of the following column.

Patrick is one course short of getting his bachelor's degree in computer science. While he is working away at that requirement, he is also employed full-time as a computer programmer. I do not know the salary range of a beginning computer programmer. In fact, I am uncertain as to what a computer programmer does to earn his money. But apparently his income is sufficient to support an apartment and a lifestyle and provide him with a certain sense of independence.

This last Christmas, he announced to his grandmother and grandfather that, after years of receiving gifts of the season, he was ready at last to reciprocate. He was going to take them out to a nice dinner whenever convenient.

Last week he escorted us to a nice little steakhouse. We had a splendid dinner, and he picked up the tab. This was the first time that anything like it had happened to us. It was an odd but nice feeling that a member of yet another generation was now assuming a responsibility. Time passes. This story may not be particularly significant, but perhaps it will stir some memories among grandparents who read this column, and maybe among even a few grandchildren now grown to adulthood.

In the spring of 1992, Alice and I took three of our grandchildren—Steve and Stephanie Boatright (accompanied by their parents) and Tiffany Harveson, youngsters who by their names would not be identified easily as of Japanese ancestry—to explore their roots in Japan. Of course, one week is not nearly enough to see the country. After a night in Tokyo, we hurried to Yamagata, where Steve was to make contact with a lad who had stayed with the Boatrights in Denver during an earlier student exchange. Then we went to Kyoto, saw the Matsushita electrical museum just outside Osaka, and took the Bullet Train to Hiroshima. The youngsters enjoyed their experience immensely, and the events of one day during the trip produced the following column on August 28.

One day in Hiroshima was all that could be spared on a hurried trip. The first half of the day was spent at the atomic bomb museum, which is the centerpiece of Peace Memorial Park. The museum was redone a few years ago, and it is still a vivid reminder of the horror of a city reduced to a radioactive wasteland by a single bomb.

In the afternoon, some of the younger members of the Fukeda family drove us out to their home in a peaceful little valley inland from Hiroshima proper. Michizume Fukeda, the patriarch, is my cousin, and I get to see him about once every five years.

On my first visit to the Fukeda home many years ago, Mrs. Fukeda told me what happened the day the bomb fell. Now I repeated that story to the grandkids as we stood in the Fukedas' front yard, looking toward the low hills that separate the home from the city.

That August morning in 1945, I said, Mrs. Fukeda was working in a rice field near her home when she was startled by an enormous thundering sound, louder than anything she had ever heard. Presently, a huge black cloud boiled into the sky on the other side of the hills, and a harsh, hot wind swept up the valley. The sky darkened. Frightened, she hurried home, where she found most of the glass broken. Even more distressing, the roof had been lifted off the walls and dropped at an angle.

Hours later, a stream of horribly burned people, blackened skin hanging from their arms, their eyes glazed, staggered up the dirt road in front of her home. Many begged for water. She helped them as best she could.

Next day, she knew what she had to do. She took her two-wheeled handcart and went into Hiroshima in search of relatives. Miraculously, she found them all, dazed but not seriously injured, and led them all back to the farmhouse where we now stood.

The grandkids listened attentively and gazed in awe at the hills that had protected the farmhouse and at Mrs. Fukeda, who is now a smiling, wrinkled grandmother, her back bent like so many elderly Japanese farm women.

When we returned to the States, I asked the grandkids what they remembered most about their ten days in Japan. Was it the astonishing hustle and bustle of Tokyo, the friendliness of folks in Yamagata, the ancient splendor of Kyoto, the speedy comfort of the Bullet Train? Osaka Castle? The *shabu-shabu* dinner or the hot springs bath? The subway rides, kamikaze taxis, or getting lost at Tokyo Station?

There was no hesitation. It was the visit to Hiroshima and learning about what happened the day the bomb fell.

As the years slipped by, *Pacific Citizen* became a more serious newspaper, concerned more with ethnic and other issues of the day than with whimsy or humor. The tone of "From the Frying Pan" changed with the times, becoming more earnest and serious and, I hope, thoughtful. But I found another outlet for the light columns I wanted to write on occasion: the *Rocky Mountain Jiho,* a tiny Denver weekly with one page of English and seven pages of Japanese. The publisher, Eiichi Imada, liked the idea of having me write a regular column to juice up a feeble English section. I called the column "Anything That Comes to Mind" and, of course, wrote anything that came to mind. What came to mind one week in 1997 was something I titled "The Story of a Piano."

My mother-in-law was a gentle, cultured woman, not unlike my own mother. She was widowed fairly early in life. Her husband published a small Japanese-language paper in Portland, Oregon, so you knew that he left few assets. His widow supported herself and her two children by working in the newspaper's print shop, by teaching in the local Japanese-language school, and giving piano lessons to young Nisei children. She was unusual in that she had studied Western music as a college student in Japan.

I am not sure, but I think my mother-in-law bought the piano before her husband died. It was an upright, of good quality, and it must have cost a large part of the family income. She was very proud of it, and she used it in her teaching.

Then came the attack on Pearl Harbor. Because my mother-in-law taught in a Japanese-language school, she automatically was classified by the FBI as a potential security risk. The gendarmes picked her up and sent her off to an enemy alien camp, even though her son was serving in the U.S. Army.

She had very few personal effects of value to take care of except for the piano. We arranged to have it stored by the piano company that had sold it to her. In time, the federal government admitted she was no security risk and let her come to live with us. When my wife and I relocated from camp to Des Moines, Iowa, she went with us, and we sent for the piano. Miraculously, it reached us virtually unscathed, and she enjoyed having it until she died.

When my wife and I moved to Denver more than fifty years ago, the piano came with us. She played it on occasion, and our two daughters took lessons and practiced on it.

Eventually, the girls grew up, married, and moved away. My wife played the piano infrequently. It was a shame to let it sit unused in the rec room, so we gave it to our elder daughter, who had learned to play quite well. In time, she had a daughter of her own, and it turned out the child, my granddaughter Stephanie, has considerable musical talent.

One recent evening Stephanie sat at her great-grandmother's piano and played for me. It was a difficult piece, advanced for a child her age, but even to my untrained ear it was evident she played it beautifully. As her fingers flew over the keyboard, she was no longer the lanky tomboy who excels at soccer and basketball. She was a budding artist, creating the beauty of music with joy and emotion.

And as I listened, I thought of her great-grandmother's love of music, the travels of her piano, and how pleased she would be to know that her great-grandchild has in some mysterious way inherited her talent and gains pleasure from an instrument that she herself treasured so long ago.

Chapter Seven

The Meaning of America

For Japanese Americans who experienced the imprisonment years, 1942–1945 is an unforgettable period. Imagine being told you are no longer entitled to the protections American citizens acquire at birth, not because of any criminal or treasonable activity, but simply because the United States is at war with the country your ancestors came from. Imagine being told that the Bill of Rights no longer applies to you, that you must leave home and job and friends and accept imprisonment, without indictment or trial, in camps behind barbed wire simply because of your race. Scholars even today debate the reason Japanese Americans accepted discrimination so passively.

But times and attitudes change. Under intense pressure from Japanese American lobbyists, Congress passed the Civil Liberties Act in 1988, and President Ronald Reagan signed it into law. In its provisions, the act expressed the nation's apology for the injustice done to Japanese Americans. President George Bush signed legislation providing each survivor with a solatium, and modest checks were distributed, along with a printed and undated letter of regret.

But for those Japanese Americans who endured internment, memories and doubts still linger. Fortunately, for most, the bitterness is long gone, if it existed in the first place. The mood of the times was captured in a poem by a young girl, Kay Masuda, which was published in the

January 1, 1943, issue of the *Sentinel,* the camp newspaper at Heart
Mountain:

Evacuee

Father, you have wronged me grievously,
I know not why you punish me
For sins not done nor reasons known,
You have caused me misery.
But through this all I look on you
As child would look on parents true,
With tenderness co-mingling in
The anguishment and bitter tears;
My heart still beats with loyalty
For you are my father.
I know no other.

If nothing else, the Evacuation engendered in me a greater concern for human rights and the Constitutional protection of those rights
under the American system. This chapter will focus on columns addressing that issue.

Pacific Citizen published the following column on January 28,
1994.

For many of us who have lived through the World War II period, the results of a Roper survey last spring on the Holocaust
are astonishing. Among other things, the survey, which sur-
faced again with the recent release of the movie *Schindler's List,*
found:

• 22% of American adults think it is possible that the Nazi program to exterminate Jews never happened, that the whole night-
marish story might have been made up.
• More than half of American high school students don't know
the meaning of the word Holocaust.
• 38% of Americans in the eighteen to twenty-nine age bracket
have no idea that Auschwitz, Dachau, and Treblinka were the
names of Nazi extermination camps.

- 14% of American high school students cannot identify the leader of the Third Reich.
- Only 35% of American adults know that some six million Jews were killed in the Holocaust.

If there is such widespread ignorance about this ghastly chapter in contemporary history, what can we expect Americans to know about the Evacuation, a comparatively infinitesimal blip in the graph lines of injustice?

That's a question likely to become increasingly significant as time passes. While I think it is safe to say that most of us don't spend time brooding about the Evacuation, for many it was the most memorable happening of their lives. The memory of its injustice, despite the nation's apology, continues to dominate the goals and activities of organizations like the Japanese American Citizens' League, a stance that is justified by the determination that nothing like it shall ever happen again.

But, in view of the brevity of human memory and reluctance to dwell on the unpleasant, for how long can it be made the focal point of the community?

It is inconceivable that there will come a time when the name of Pearl Harbor will draw blank stares from young Americans. Today the memory is kept alive by the survivors of both the event and the era, with the support of the media and the political leadership. But time passes. Today we seldom give thought to the sacrifices of those who went to Europe in 1917–1918 in the futile mission to make the world safe for democracy, nor do we remember the *Maine.* We have a hard time recalling the reasons for the Gulf War, much less Vietnam, Korea, and the bloody little skirmishes in between, such as the Kent State massacre and the Democratic Convention head- and window bashing in Chicago.

If the horror and scale of the Holocaust have left such little impression on the consciousness of succeeding generations, our efforts to perpetuate the memory of the Evacuation may be like whistling into the wind. Still, wouldn't it be a betrayal of our commitment to justice if we didn't continue to try?

A somewhat similar theme, pegged to current events, appears in a column published on July 11, 1986.

It isn't good manners to throw rocks at a birthday party where everyone is having a grand time and the mood is exhilaratingly upbeat. So I hope you will understand when I point out, without rancor, a certain insensitivity in the New York celebration of the 100th birthday of Miss Liberty and the 210th birthday of the United States.

The celebration centered on the restoration of the Statue of Liberty. This is entirely proper, since the vast majority of immigrants who populated and helped make our country what it is were Europeans who entered through the port of New York, and the first meaningful sight of their new lives was the Statue of Liberty.

But Europeans were not the only immigrants, and my complaint is based on the perception that the others—notably the blacks, the Hispanics, and the Asians—were largely slighted in the effort to give the celebration a national dimension.

The blacks arrived not in the shining light of the "lamp beside the golden door," but in chains in the holds of stinking slave ships. And as I wrote in the book *Nisei:* "There wasn't even a Statue of Liberty—nor has anyone ever seriously suggested there ought to be one—to hold aloft a lamp of hope for the benefit of Asian immigrants beside the Golden Gate or any other Pacific portal."

Regardless of the circumstances of their arrival, blacks, Asians, and others have contributed mightily to the progress and prosperity of the United States. They accomplished this in the face not of encouragement and welcome, but hostility and often violent opposition.

There were, to be sure, a few heartwarming gestures of recognition for Asians during the New York festivities. I. M. Pei, the architect, and An Wang, the computer whiz, both Chinese immigrants, were among those presented the prestigious Medal of Liberty. Hue Cao, an eleven-year-old Vietnamese refugee now living in Hawaii, read her prizewinning essay about the meaning of freedom. And there were a few Asian faces visible in brief views of the newest naturalized Americans.

But for those who have been concerned with the equal sharing of Constitutional rights, it was not a little disturbing that platitudes were voiced without recognition that liberty and justice were not served to all on a silver platter. There was struggle involved in the claiming of rights guaranteed by the nation's basic documents, as the blacks know, and we Japanese Americans know.

Perhaps a celebration of the triumph of American democracy is not the time to wear a hair shirt as a confession of grievous faults, but unfortunately Liberty's birthday party also turned out to be a demonstration of the national willingness to sweep shortcomings under the rug.

It would have been more sensitive and inspiring if the nation, instead of spending so much time in self-congratulatory extolling of its virtues, had pledged to redouble its efforts to put into practice the higher ideals that, too often, have been only paper pledges subject to the disgrace of bigotry.

Then, on September 20, 1991, I commented on what I considered another lost opportunity, amid the euphoria of self-adulation, to face up to the shortcomings in our democracy.

The 200th anniversary of the ratification of the Bill of Rights— "the heart and soul of our liberty," as someone described it—is being celebrated this year. In observation of the event, the Philip Morris companies are sponsoring a nationwide tour of an exhibit that features one of the twelve known remaining original copies.

I went to see the exhibit when it came to Denver and was both moved and disappointed. Moved because of the document's significance in the history of civilization. Disappointed because no mention was made of the devastating assault on the Bill of Rights in 1942 that demonstrated what a fragile document it is without the constant vigilance and support of the people.

That vigilance and support vanished in the war hysteria that followed Japan's attack on Pearl Harbor. Ten weeks later, the civil rights guaranteed by the Bill of Rights were suspended for 120,000 members of a racial minority—two-thirds of them citizens by birth—by the signing of a presidential executive order. They were herded into detention camps without being accused of anything other than that they were of the same racial stock as the Japanese enemy.

Few of their fellow citizens protested. Few realized that when the rights of some are violated, the rights of all are endangered. That is the lesson the Philip Morris exhibit should have underscored, and failed to do. Instead, the exhibit focused simply on reminding citizens what a precious document the Bill of Rights is.

But the reality is that the principles enunciated in the Bill of Rights are meaningless unless the people demand that they be applied. This did not happen in 1942. For example:

The Fifth Amendment states that no person shall be "deprived of life, liberty, or property, without due process of law." Soldiers with bayonets, not due process, forced Japanese Americans from their homes and into detention camps.

The Sixth Amendment provides that "in all criminal prosecutions, the accused shall enjoy the right to a speedy and public trial . . . and to be informed of the nature and cause of the accusations."

It can be argued that "criminal prosecution" was not involved in the imprisonment of Japanese Americans. True, they were not charged with any crime. They were simply accused, en masse, of being a potential danger to the national security because of race. They were imprisoned without trial in an effort to thwart that potential danger, but at what violence to the Bill of Rights?

The Fourteenth Amendment repeats the Fifth Amendment's provision for "due process" and further provides that no person shall be denied "the equal protection of the laws." The laws were not applied equally to an American minority that simply had a physical resemblance to the hated enemy.

Some contend that guaranteed freedoms may have to be suspended temporarily in a national emergency, such as war, but the argument rings hollow when the suspension is applied selectively on a racial basis, as it was in 1942.

The freedoms embraced by the Bill of Rights are basic concepts, but they are not simple. They are strongly idealistic but at the same time frail without public understanding and determination to preserve them.

One additional point. The First Amendment guarantees the right of the people "to petition the government for a redress of grievances." Many years after their imprisonment, Japanese Americans set out in search of redress. Under their prodding, Congress in 1988 passed a law calling for restitution and apology to Japanese Americans. It was signed by President Reagan. Less than a year ago, President Bush formalized the apology with a renewed "commitment to the ideals of freedom, equality, and justice."

Thus a democracy demonstrated it could correct its errors.

This is the lesson that the Philip Morris exhibit should have brought to Americans. In glorifying the ideals but ignoring the realities, the project fell short. It was glitzy and shallow, like so much of our civilization these days, and a great opportunity to promote better understanding of our democracy was lost.

We must not underestimate the curiosity of citizens about the past, nor fail to satisfy that desire for information. I addressed this matter in a column published on September 18, 1992.

Fifty years—a half century—after the Evacuation, has the time come to put that deplorable event behind us? Has the time come to put aside the unforgettable and go on to other things?

Well, fortunately, most of us went on to other things long ago, rearing families, working for a living, seeking whatever enjoyment there is to be found in life, and making our small contributions to society.

But recently, after visiting a local high school class, I was reminded afresh that the memory of the Evacuation needs to be kept alive. I'd like to share with you excerpts from letters the students sent me after I talked with them about the Japanese American experience:

"Thank you for coming to our school and telling us what it was like for you during the war. I learned a lot about how it was in the concentration camps."

"Some of the things you said I took to heart because I know how you must have felt when you were in this camp."

"The things you said were very sad and almost unthinkable to do to someone. I could expect that to be in a movie and not in real life."

"You have a lot of very interesting facts and I learned a lot."

"It made me think about how other people treat people just because of their skin color or ethnic background. It's really sad to know how your people were treated."

"I learned stuff I didn't know."

This last is exactly the point—to teach kids stuff they didn't know about human rights and the sanctity of the Constitution and what happens when people get excited and forget about principles that govern our country.

Their teachers know, if only vaguely, what happened to a then unpopular Japanese American minority in 1942. They could tell their students about that episode, but then that would be just another classroom lecture, with no particular impact. But if someone who had firsthand experience could be enticed to come to class and talk to the kids, now that would make them sit up and listen. So history teachers and social science teachers look for former evacuees who would be willing to give up an hour to come to class and talk about their experiences.

A long time ago, a doddering old Civil War veteran came to my grade school class and talked about what it had been like during the War Between the States. I don't remember the details of what he said, but I do recall that he stirred an interest that I satisfied by going to the library and picking up books about that time.

It's just a bit demoralizing to think that I am now cast in the role of a doddering old witness to history, helping kids to remember what was and is important to us Americans.

"The Evacuation was a sad episode in America's history which deserves to be remembered," the teacher wrote in a note accompanying the letters from the students.

If I can help kids learn and remember, then it's an hour well spent.

When you put more than 100,000 men, women, and children in cold storage, it is wise to have a pretty good reason for doing so. Unfortunately, members of the Japanese American community were interned in camps or imprisoned based on any intelligence—the word is used in the broadest sense—that an informer could dredge up. A responsible agency would sift through this raw hearsay, evaluate it for reliability by checking it against other sources, and make a considered judgment. This was not done. The rationalization for this sorry state of affairs was that urgent national security interests made it imprudent to delay action. What's worse, much of the raw, unevaluated, unconfirmed, and often slanderous information still is filed away in the archives, available to anyone invoking the Freedom of Information Act. When I learned of this, I wrote the following column on November 3, 1995.

You are a Sansei, middle-aged whether you want to admit it or not, well established in your profession and with time now to think occasionally about your heritage as a Japanese American.

You are a Yonsei, fresh out of college and starting in a career that was closed by discriminatory barriers to your Nisei grandparents. Or perhaps you are an upperclassman at a prestigious university where your history or sociology courses touch on the Asian American experience.

Whoever you may be, and whatever the reasons, you begin to remember vaguely the stories your parents or grandparents or even great-grandparents told about the "olden" days when they lived and worked in Li'l Tokyo enclaves or on tiny truck farms. And other stories about the Great Migration under military orders into inland concentration camps during the long-ago war between the United States and Japan.

You begin to wish you had paid closer attention to those stories, that you remembered more about them. And now, because you are curious or because you want to write a term paper, you read some of the dozens of books that have been written about your people. And as you probe deeper, you learn that there is something called the Freedom of Information Act, which enables ordinary citizens like you to request documents buried in the archives of government agencies—agencies like the Federal Bureau of Investigation, naval and army intelligence, the War Relocation Authority. And you're curious about what, if anything, the documents say about your relatives who went through the Evacuation because of suspected mass disloyalty.

So you write to these agencies (although WRA was absorbed by the Interior Department and no longer exists), cite the Freedom of Information Act, and ask for documents about specific individuals. Eventually, the authorities send you copies of a few documents, poorly reproduced from microfilm and sometimes barely legible.

And what you read is likely to be an astonishing collection of misinformation, unsupported innuendo, and equally unsupported charges of subversion and disloyalty. Here and there, a name, obviously that of an informer, will be inked out, but in most instances you will find no source for the libel.

Not long ago, I saw a 1945 naval intelligence report, stamped "Confidential," which described without attribution various persons identified by name and city of residence as being "a threat to security of U.S.," "reported to be definitely pro-Japanese," "disloyal to U.S." and deceitful and crooked, "un-American," "regarded as the No. 1 objectionable Japanese." Ad nauseum.

There is no indication of who filed this report, or the sources of information used to compile it. This slanderous, unproven information reposes in government archives available to anyone who asks for a copy. The government hands out this material with no disclaimer whatever. There is no statement, not even a hint, that the information in the files was from unidentified sources, nor that history has proven much of it to be false, if not malicious. The cruelty lives on, preserved apparently for all time and open for public view. Can anything be more un-American?

On a somewhat related subject, I wrote the following column on August 18, 1995.

By the time this column is published, the furor over former defense secretary Robert McNamara's book [*In Retrospect* (Times Books, 1995)], confessing his error in pursuing the Vietnam War long after he realized how wrong it was, will have died away. But there exists a somewhat parallel situation that is made timely by McNamara's admission.

That would be the Evacuation, followed by internment, a devastating chapter of history opened when President Franklin D. Roosevelt signed Executive Order 9066, which authorized the imprisoning of an American minority based on race. The authority for the mass ouster of citizens from their homes had been requested by Secretary of War Henry L. Stimson. Congress did nothing to block it. Later it was ruled a legal action by the United States Supreme Court.

Yet, in more recent times, there have been second thoughts about the decision to remove and imprison Japanese Americans in violation of their Constitutional rights as a wartime security measure. Presidents Bush and Reagan have apologized for it. At various times, presidents Truman, Ford, and Carter have deplored it. Congress approved a measure to redress the wrong.

But none of these people was responsible for the Evacuation in the way McNamara was responsible for the American role in the Vietnam War. The officials involved pivotally in the Evacuation in much the same way that McNamara was involved in Vietnam were Lieutenant General John L. DeWitt, Lieutenant General Allen W. Gullion (a somewhat mysterious figure behind the scenes), Colonel Karl R. Bendetsen, and the assistant secretary of war, John J. McCloy.

Several personalities involved less directly—Stimson, Attorney General Francis Biddle, the then California attorney general and later governor and chief justice of the Supreme Court Earl Warren—have expressed regret about the Evacuation in their biographies, but only briefly, as though the episode was only a minor event in their lives.

DeWitt has had to take much of the blame for the Evacuation decisions, but history seems to show he was pretty much the figurehead who signed the papers placed on his desk by a far stronger character, Bendetsen. Both are now dead, as is McCloy.

But during the redress hearings, McCloy and Bendetsen testified that they thought they were doing what was best for their country in pressing for the evacuation of all Japanese Americans from the West Coast, and in similar circumstances today, they would issue the same orders. In other words, unlike McNamara, they were unrepentant. In the glare of the hearings called by the Commission on Wartime Relocation and Internment of Citizens, there wasn't much else they dared say.

Thus there is no authoritative person alive today to come forward, as McNamara has done, to admit error and offer apology.

Yet one wonders if in their hearts, in the quiet of the night, Bendetsen and McCloy had some doubts about their decision in the face of the Constitution they had sworn to uphold. McNamara has had to face some savage criticism, but at least he had the courage to reveal what he believed.

There is also evidence that in early 1944, President Roosevelt was advised that there was no danger of the Japanese invading the U.S. West Coast, and therefore no reason not to let the Japanese Americans return to their homes. But those around him counseled that in view of the upcoming election campaign, it would be unwise to stir up the West Coast electorate by allowing the "Japanese" to return. So they remained imprisoned for another year.

American political miscreants were not the only ones I took to task. The following column was published March 26, 1993, after a particularly irritating incident.

About the nicest thing that can be said of Masao Kokubo is that he is ignorant, insensitive, and stupid.

Kokubo, member of the prefectural assembly in Hyogo prefecture in western Japan, is the latest Japanese politician who unzipped his mouth when he should have been thinking.

According to the Associated Press, which picked up the item from Japan's Kyodo News Service, Kokubo told a budget committee meeting last week that Japanese "feel tainted when they shake hands with a black person."

"We know in our heads that discrimination is bad, but our feelings are different," Kokubo was quoted.

"When you shake hands with someone who is completely black, you feel your hands getting black."

In this manner did Kokubo join the pantheon of Japanese political dunces: Justice Minister Seiroku Kajiyama, who compared the arrival of foreign prostitutes in Japan to blacks moving into all-white neighborhoods in the U.S.; former House speaker Yoshio Sakurauchi, who said Japan was superior to the U.S. because American workers were illiterate and lazy; and whoever—unfortunately the name escapes me at the moment—blamed blacks who don't pay their debts for the problems of the American economy. It is small consolation to realize that American politicians aren't the only ones who put their mouths in motion without getting their brains in gear.

Kokubo was talking about Pakistani and Asian Indian laborers who have come into Japan seeking jobs that pay better than at home. But American blacks quickly, and rightly, took umbrage. In Denver, one black spokesman threatened to picket a Japan America Society (an organization dedicated to better understanding between peoples of the two countries) function unless there was an immediate apology. It seemed to make no difference to the irate spokesman that members of the Japan America Society were as outraged as he by Kokubo's remarks.

This kind of assumption of guilt by association is an extremely unfortunate part of problems involving relations between Japan and the United States. Of course, the most obvious example is the Japanese attack on Pearl Harbor. Within hours, the resulting anger was being directed irrationally at Japanese Americans.

When U.S.–Japan trade disputes heat up, again it is the Japanese Americans who often are tagged for blame. At this writing, it is too early to see how Kokubo's insensitivity will play, but certainly the reaction is unlikely to be minor. Kokubo can apologize—the Japanese are good at that—but the damage has been done. We have every right to be angry that Kokubo is so ignorant of the potential damage his remarks can cause.

No country and no people have a monopoly on insensitivity and stupidity, and Americans have been as guilty as anyone in this area. But such actions are particularly hurtful when they affect us Japanese Americans who happen to be regarded as people of color. Kokubo should know better. He needs to be told so in no uncertain terms by both Americans and Japanese, as well as all people of color.

Fortunately for U.S.–Japanese relations, Kokubo's faux pas had no lasting impact and was soon forgotten. Unfortunately, it probably will not be the last of gratuitous insults voiced by unthinking public figures on both sides of the Pacific Ocean.

Lest we leave the impression that all politicians are dunces, I want to tell you about Ralph L. Carr, who was governor of Colorado in 1942 when the feds first began talking about ousting all Japanese Americans from the West Coast and locking them up in inland detention camps. Following is my column of October 4, 1996.

I don't think it is stretching matters to suggest that a statement written by Ralph L. Carr as governor of Colorado deserves the kind of recognition now reserved for President Lincoln's Gettysburg Address.

You don't know of Ralph Carr? Shame. Let me tell you. Carr was the only Western governor to remember the Constitution when others were hysterically demanding imprisonment of all Japanese Americans in the early days of the war. This is what he wrote:

"When it is suggested that American citizens be thrown into concentration camps, where they lose all the privileges of citizenship under the Constitution, then the principles of that great document are violated and lost. If a man may be deprived of his liberty . . . without proof of misconduct, without the filing of charges, and without a hearing, simply because men now living in the country where his grandfather was born have become the active enemies of the United States, then we are disregarding the very principles for which this war is being waged against the Axis nations."

At a meeting of Western governors in Salt Lake City on the eve of the Evacuation, Carr alone said Japanese Americans as refugees from the West Coast would be welcome in his state. He knew the political consequences of his stand for decency. So hated were the Japanese Americans that his career in politics was finished.

More than a half century later, the people of Colorado took note of this historic episode. Three bronze tablets were mounted on the east lawn of the Capitol on a sunny September noon. One carries the above quotation from Carr, "a Colorado native, a lawyer and a preeminent citizen of Colorado whose statesmanship and political courage transcend time and place."

The second tells the story of the Amache detention camp, the Evacuation, and the Japanese Americans in military service. "Their valor reflected uncommon strength of character and great faith in this nation of immigrants," the plaque says. "They and their families have enriched our country beyond measure."

And the third states simply that the tablets are a remembrance of Governor Ralph L. Carr "and those Americans who passed through the gates of Amache." The tablet also notes that the sponsors are the Colorado Bar Association, the Japanese American community, and the citizens of Colorado.

Japanese Americans did indeed contribute generously of time and money to the project, particularly members of the Asian American Bar Association. But they weren't the principal advocates. It is significant and heartwarming that the main thrust for the project came from outside the ethnic community—the Colorado Bar Association and the State Legislature. I don't think it is too outlandish to say that on a modest scale, what happened in Colorado would be somewhat comparable to the American Bar Association and Congress taking the initiative in providing redress—an apology from the government and token compensation for an official wrong. But in that case, the American Bar Association paid no attention, and Congress kicked and screamed before passing legislation for redress.

Chapter Eight

A Bicultural Diet

A merican cuisine has been enriched by the infusion of various international foods and methods of food preparation. (In fact, American culture as a whole has benefited tremendously from exposure to other cultures.) French cooking has added a certain elegance and a variety of sauces, as well as rich and exotic cheeses. The Italians brought with them pastas of many shapes and provided a savory use for overripe tomatoes. Thank Germany for tasty sausages. Mexican fare performs wonders with beans, corn, and spices, and Mexican restaurants seem as plentiful as the truly native American fast-food hamburger and chicken emporiums. Hungarians are alleged to be the originators of goulash. And although it has been said that chop suey was the invention of a black cook in a small Harlem restaurant, Chinese food (of often uncertain quality) seems to be available in any American community of more than 15,000 residents. Unfortunately, the rich delights of true Chinese cuisine can be found only in a few major cities.

It should be noted, however, that some ethnic dishes have not caught the interest of American palates, among them lutefisk, a Norwegian delicacy of fish treated with lye; gefilte fish, of Yiddish origins; and Scotland's haggis, in which various ingredients are cooked together in the stomach of a sheep.

Many Japanese immigrants, weary of railroad or farm labor, opened restaurants in the 1920s, when they had saved up a little money. Most of these featured only simple, standard American cooking—ham and eggs, pancakes, meat loaf, hamburger steak, beef stew, pork chops, corned beef and cabbage, ham and fried egg sandwiches, apple pie, bread pudding, and other traditional fare that did not require great culinary skill. The popularity and availability of Japanese cuisine—other than the ubiquitous sukiyaki—is largely a postwar phenomenon.

It may seem passing strange that the cuisine of the hated Japanese enemy of World War II should gain such impressive favor among Americans. On the other hand, American servicemen in Occupied Japan may have, to borrow from an advertising slogan, tried it and liked it. In any event, blocks of white, soft, tasteless tofu, made from soybeans, landed on American tables some decades after war's end, followed by slices of uncooked fish. Raw fish? (Retching sound.) That was the first reaction, but before long, sushi bars were proliferating and prospering. On May 31, 1985, I wrote:

> Some weeks ago, a Denver newspaper columnist wrote a supercilious (that means snotty) piece about sushi. Ugh, he said in effect. Raw fish. How horrible. How disgusting. He wouldn't be caught putting that kind of yucky stuff in his mouth.
>
> That writer must have been reared on meat and potatoes, or maybe hamburgers and fries, or more probably sow belly, mustard greens, and grits. Nothing wrong with such fare, but there are other interesting foods available in America these days.
>
> What started his dinner table tantrum was a syndicated news story warning that eating raw fish could result in intestinal worms. What he didn't bother to find out was that sushi is not synonymous with sashimi, and many kinds of sushi don't use raw fish. Nor did his research, minimal if any, reveal that over the centuries, the Japanese have learned to use only varieties of fish resistant to infection for sashimi. Parenthetically, it should be noted that the occasional *E. coli* scares in the U.S., blamed on unsanitary processing of chicken and beef, horrifies Japanese.
>
> Then, the other day, Ruth Tanbara of St. Paul, Minnesota, sent along a copy of a column from one of the Twin Cities papers based on the same raw-fish-causes-worms dispatch, and

repeating the canard about sashimi. In addition, the columnist expressed astonishment, if that is the word, that the Japanese eat the puffer, or blowfish, "whose incredibly toxic flesh is also served raw in a dish called fugu."

Two things wrong there, fella. It's not the flesh that's toxic, but certain organs. And it's the fish that's called fugu, not the dish. The Minnesota columnist confirms my contention that newspaper pundits are generically lazy, and in times of desperate search for an idea, which is often, they will embrace anything that can be made to fill the space. I know. I've done it. Often.

But take it from one who has partaken of fugu. The flesh is (1) not toxic and (2) not particularly tasty. Fugu sashimi is so bland it has to be jazzed up with a sauce of lemon and soy sauce and other stuff to make it interesting. Give me fresh filet of raw tuna anytime over fugu, which I consider to be overrated as gourmet fare.

Fugu's fascination for the Japanese seems to be that it offers an opportunity to pretend they are playing Russian roulette while sipping warm sake and singing rowdy songs off-key. If the chef happened to be nursing a hangover and punctured the dangerous organ while preparing the fish, it could be *sayonara* for the customers. This almost never happens but is guaranteed to get lots of newspaper space when it does.

Some Japanese who consider fugu a delicacy turn pale when they learn the nature of Rocky Mountain oysters—the product of castrating cattle—which residents of the American West feel obliged to push on outsiders along with snickers and wise looks. Fortunately, the custom is not to eat Rocky Mountain oysters chilled and raw, but to coat them with bread crumbs or flour and fry them thoroughly before serving, which effectively camouflages the taste.

But getting back to tofu, I wrote the following column on March 22, 1985.

My *Merriam Webster Third International Dictionary,* a massive tome of more than 2,660 pages, contains the word *tofu* but not *sushi*. My edition was copyrighted in 1971, which was back in the days when most red-blooded Americans would screw up their faces in disgust and cry, "Oooh, yuck," at the thought of eating cold rice topped by a slice of raw fish.

Times change. A Japanese restaurant is hardly a Japanese restaurant these days without a sushi bar where patrons cheerfully consume $20 worth of sushi as a light snack to go with their beer. And tofu, once a plebeian food manufactured from the lowly soybean and that still provides much of the protein intake of people in meat-short parts of Asia, now appears in high-priced American ice cream, salads, desserts, and even hamburgers.

By itself, tofu is as flavorsome as cottage cheese or curds and whey. But it has a way of adapting to its culinary environment, which makes tofu palatable when taken straight in a soy sauce dip or, heaven forbid, gooped up with honey and sugar in a blender.

The current issue of *Tokyo Newsletter,* published by the Mitsubishi Corporation, has a cover story on tofu, which is called "traditional food for a post-industrial society."

The article, by Masanobu Gabe (pronounced Gah-Beh), says tofu probably was invented some 2,000 years ago by a Chinese philosopher, Wang Liu-an, grandson of the founder of the Han dynasty, and introduced to Japan about 1,000 years ago.

Tofu plays such a large part in the Japanese diet that there's even a Japan Federation of Tofu and Aburage (fried tofu) Commerce and Industry Association. Its secretary-general, says author Gabe, estimates the average Japanese household consumes 120 cakes of tofu a year, manufactured by 26,800 companies.

When I was a youngster growing up in Seattle, tofu was delivered by a fellow in a panel truck from a dark, dank backroom factory to Japanese grocery stores in five-gallon tins filled with water. Today, one firm in Japan uses four tons of soybeans daily to make 50,000 cakes of tofu delivered by refrigerator trucks.

Gabe tells us that more than 90 percent of the soybeans Japan uses for tofu are grown in the United States, with beans from Indiana, Ohio, and Michigan reputed to be the best. Commodore Perry is credited with bringing back the first soybean seeds from Japan in 1854. Japan grows only about 230,000 tons of the approximately 120 million tons consumed annually in the various products of soybeans. Of course, there are old-timers who contend there's nothing like the tofu that was made in the good old days from real Japanese soybeans, but those days are gone forever. Author Gabe also tells us that tofu may have been the first freeze-dried food. It's *koridofu,* also called *koyadofu,* developed by Buddhist priests in a monastery on, naturally, Mount Koya. Today, in a fully automated process, the tofu is frozen, allowed to cure, then thawed and dried.

To me the product is the consistency of, and about as palatable as, a DuPont synthetic sponge. But I will not hold it against you if you like *koyadofu.* Each person to his tastes. There's nothing quite so refreshing as chilled tofu served with soy sauce and a bit of grated ginger on a hot summer day, and thank you, Commodore Perry, for bringing back those seeds.

A few weeks after that column was published, I received a letter from my friend Jack Maki—the one who had alerted me to the attack on Pearl Harbor. By then, he had retired from his teaching position at the University of Massachusetts. He said, in part:

Your reference to Perry and the soybean struck a responsive chord in me, for I have been interested in the question for some time. I had not heard of the Perry connection, and so I checked my copy of his long and fascinating report.

The only reference is to a "peculiar, hairy-podded bean" and another lentil-type bean, from one of which, the report says, soy sauce is made. Also soybeans are not included in the long, long list of dried botanical specimens that Perry brought back. Unless more evidence is supplied, I am rather dubious that Perry brought back the seeds.

Recently, E. J. Kahn Jr. had a series of fascinating articles in the *New Yorker* magazine on the world's staple foods. One dealt with soybeans. Kahn writes that Benjamin Franklin brought (or

sent) the first seeds from Paris—he was the U.S. ambassador—
where they had been brought from China. You may recall that
there was a great fad for things Chinese in Europe in the 18th
Century.

My own interest originated in an article written a number of
years ago which credited William P. Brooks with the introduction of soybeans as a crop into this country in the 1880s. Brooks
was of the class of 1875 at Massachusetts Agricultural College
(now University of Massachusetts) who went to Japan to join
William Smith Clark who went out in 1876 to open Sapporo Agricultural College, now Hokkaido University.

I conclude that Perry was obviously the first American to report on soybeans as a Japanese bean, Ben Franklin introduced
the first seeds, and Brooks was responsible for their introduction as an American-raised crop.

Okay, okay.

In addition to tofu, soybeans can be eaten in a variety of ways. Boiled
in the pod in salt water, soybeans serve the same purpose as peanuts at
your favorite watering place. You pick up a pod, squeeze it gently in front
of your face, and a bean pops out of the pod and into your mouth. I returned to the subject of soybeans June 4, 1993, in the following column.

Before they began using a lot of dairy products, the Japanese, during the U.S. Occupation, complained that Americans
were *batah-kusai*—that they stank of butter. I don't know
whether this is true. In any event, now that the Japanese themselves use plenty of butter on their bread (made of U.S. wheat),
eat cheese, and drink coffee with cream, the smell of butter
doesn't seem to bother them.

Compared to butter or anything else, the Japanese diet in-
cludes some foods whose odor is truly world-class. For example,
I am thinking of *takuwan,* which is pickled daikon, which in
turn is giant white radish.

What brought this up?

Well, the other day I saw a feature in a Japanese magazine
about the delights of an old-time dish called *natto,* which is re-

gaining some popularity. It is a traditional delicacy, if that is the proper word, relished by many despite its plebeian nature and an utterly repulsive appearance.

Never heard of *natto?* Hold your nose while I tell you about it. Its main ingredient is the versatile soybean, which also makes tofu as well as plastic, paint, and other inedibles. The soybeans, according to the magazine story, are boiled, then wrapped in straw and left to ferment in a warm place for a few days.

Presently, the soybeans develop slime as well as a pungent aroma. The magazine reports that refined Japanese shunned the word *natto* but referred to it as *ito* (thread) because of the delicate, stringy white nature of the slime.

Natto is now available commercially in small packages. The fermented beans can be added to miso soup. Or they can be mixed with onions and soy sauce and poured over a bowl of hot rice, somewhat like tomato sauce over pasta. Because the mess by its nature is slippery, it is not considered bad manners to slurp the rice.

The article reports that *natto,* while once looked on as a very inelegant food, is now stocked in many grocery stores, and it is served in some first-class hotels. "Natto's renewed popularity is probably linked to growing health consciousness among Japan's aging population," the magazine says without further explanation.

I suppose natto as a delicacy is no more strange than the gristle in pickled pigs' feet, the mold in Roquefort cheese, blood sausage and headcheese, calf's brain omelet, chitlins, sweetbreads, and some other items I'd rather not mention that are part of the cuisine of the West.

If you encounter some natto at your favorite sushi bar and have the courage to try it, along with sea urchin eggs, warty green sea cucumber (not a vegetable), and other uncooked oddities, I hope you'll tell me what you think.

Soybeans can be fermented and made into a paste called miso, which is about the consistency of peanut butter and has a variety of culinary uses, including as a base for soup. I did not consider miso likely to become a favorite candidate for flavoring American cooking, but I was mistaken. On February 16, 1990, I wrote:

In Sushi and Sourdough, his recent book about the Japanese in Alaska, Tooru Kanazawa tells about the way meals were served in the salmon cannery bunkhouses. The tables were not large, and to save space, boiled rice was piled into dishpans that were slipped into crude wire frames suspended about forehead high with cords from the ceiling. You simply reached out and served yourself when you needed another bowl of rice—which for teenage cannery hands was often.

I remember those times well. There wasn't much variety to what you ate with the rice because the labor contractors weren't in business to be generous. Usually it was salmon, grilled or baked, three times a day, plus a cooked vegetable like Chinese cabbage. And miso soup served in dingy, chipped lacquer bowls.

Miso soup with meals was as inevitable as salmon. I discovered early that no matter how it is made, there is something repulsive-looking about miso soup. Miso, which is a concoction of fermented soybeans, has an unpleasant bilious color that makes the soup look like a potion of brown clay dissolved in swamp water.

My fellow Nisei laborers professed to hate miso soup, and so, early on, I decided I didn't like it either. Perhaps it was the monotony of miso soup for three meals every day. Perhaps it was the way it looked. Actually, the taste isn't half bad, and after I didn't have to have miso soup regularly, I came to enjoy it.

I got to thinking about all this the other evening while at a Japanese restaurant. There were two youngish Caucasian couples at an adjoining table, and I overheard the waitress offering them a choice of clear or miso soup before the entree. All four chose miso.

If anyone had suggested to our cannery mess hall many decades ago that someday white-skinned Americans would be consuming miso soup by choice, there would have been hoots of disagreement and derision.

I don't know what brought about change. There was a time when the only seafood familiar to many Americans was canned salmon or salt cod. Catholics were derided as "mackerel-snappers," and the thought of eating fish raw would turn people pale. Not anymore. It's a hick town these days that doesn't have a sushi restaurant, and few of them would survive on Japanese or Japanese American patronage alone. (As a matter of fact, prices are such that most Nisei can afford sushi only infrequently.) And they're brewing soy sauce, which we used to call bug-juice, in the conservative American Midwest for sale in supermarkets nationwide.

There's been a furor about Japanese purchase of American real estate, the inroads Japanese cars have made into Detroit's domain, and the predominance of Japanese-made electronic goods. But we haven't heard much about the growing popularity of Japanese food as a change of pace from such traditional American dishes as tacos, spaghetti, and chow mein. When Americans show a preference for miso soup, it's something that deserves attention.

Apropos of miso soup, I heard a young Japanese American ask with a twinkle in his eye, "Did you know Jesus is Japanese?" I took the bait and asked why. "Because he loves me so (miso)."

Frankly, the meals we got at home as youngsters were quite ordinary and often monotonous. Going out to eat, which happened infrequently, meant going to a Chinese restaurant. That was a major treat. And because none of the Japanese restaurants in Seattle were large enough to accommodate a banquet, the community's festive functions were held in Chinese restaurants. The memory of those meals led to this next column, published on April 27, 1984.

We took some of the kids and grandchildren out for a Chinese dinner the other night, and the way they put away the food stirred memories of what it was like when our folks would take us out.

Chinese chow was a great treat back in those days, just as it is today. There's nothing quite as bad as poorly prepared Chinese food, and nothing as quite as good as the very best.

There were three main Japanese-operated Chinese restaurants in the Seattle of my youth—Gyokko Ken, Nikko Low, and Kinka Low. (Isn't it remarkable that we should remember their names when so much else has faded away?) We didn't discover until we'd grown up, and made some friends among Chinese Americans, that there were even better restaurants in Chinatown.

The Issei had their own generic terms for Chinese food—China-meshi, Shina-meshi, Nankin'-meshi, or just plain chop suey. The Japanese-operated Chinese restaurants named above were the scene of some memorable banquets as well as family dinners. They served enormous quantities of food, and my recollection is that all of it was delicious.

Those were the days when our appetites were immense. The rice was served in oversized bowls, at least 50 percent and maybe 100 percent larger than the ordinary rice bowls we used at home. For some reason, it was necessary to eat rice along with the egg foo yung, the sweet-and-sour spareribs, the pineapple chicken, the bean curd and pork, and the other dishes that were staples of those Chinese meals. The rice was bland and the rest of the food rich, and somehow they complemented each other. In their prime, some of the guys could put away as many as five bowls of rice along with heaping helpings of the trimmings. Ah, memories.

In the last few years, following the influx of large numbers of immigrants from Taiwan, Hong Kong, Vietnam, and the mainland, an astonishing number of Chinese restaurants have sprung up all over the United States.

We used to have nothing but Cantonese-style cooking because the first Chinese immigrants were Cantonese and many of them went into the restaurant business. But the later arrivals brought with them skills in Peking-style cooking, the peppery Szechuan dishes, and the delightful Shanghai cuisine. And so Americans discovered that Chinese cooking wasn't simply chop suey and chow mein.

Still, it is difficult not to compare the "new" Chinese dishes with the relatively plain fare served in the Chinese restaurants of boyhood. What we used to have, compared to what is available now, must have been rather ordinary. But memory tells us it was wonderfully tasty food, perhaps because our taste buds were sharper then, and our appetites seldom were fully satisfied during the growing years.

Someday, perhaps, the grandkids will remember back to the meals we shared, and I hope their recollections will be as warm as those of my own boyhood. There's nothing like a good Chinese meal for stirring good thoughts and old memories.

I returned to the subject of Chinese food in a 1996 column in the Rocky Mountain Jiho. It illustrates, I think, the longevity of memories about special foods.

In recent years, it seems the nature of Chinese food has changed everything in the U.S. of A. Now we're getting Peking-style, or Hunan-style, or Shanghai-style, or with Vietnamese accents, and while it's mostly good, none of it seems to compare with the Cantonese dishes that we knew on the West Coast.

This, according to the lady of my household, is particularly true of sweet-and-sour spareribs, which was called pakkui or pakkai, depending on the part of the Pacific Coast where you lived. The ribs were cooked up with chunks of canned pineapple, but it was the thick brown gravy that distinguished it.

We have not been able to find brown-gravy sweet-and-sour spareribs in these parts. The restaurants have sweet-and-sour ribs, all right, but it's always covered with bright red gravy. And red gravy is different from brown gravy, not only in appearance but most definitely in flavor.

Not long ago we visited Portland, Oregon, which, prewar, rivaled San Francisco for the excellence of its Chinese food. Now we had hopes that at least some of the Chinese restaurants we had known were still in business and still serving the old-style Cantonese dishes, in particular sweet-and-sour spareribs with brown gravy.

One of our hosts, made aware of our anticipation, set out to find a restaurant that favored brown gravy. He must have telephoned a half dozen restaurants with the same question: do you have sweet-and-sour pork with brown gravy?

All of them said no, their gravy was red. Finally, he called a Chinese friend from prewar days. She said only the old restaurants had ribs with brown gravy, and she suggested the Hung Far Low in Chinatown, which had been a big prewar favorite but hadn't kept up with the times.

Of course we remembered the Hung Far Low. Who could forget a name like that, with its somewhat suggestive implications? Anyway, our friend called the restaurant, and they said yes, their sweet-and-sour spareribs had brown gravy on them.

So we went to the Hung Far Low and had, among other dishes, sweet-and-sour ribs. Ah, yes. The brown gravy was far superior to red gravy, even though there were no chunks of canned pineapple.

I'm sorry we didn't get the recipe. It would have been fun to try it at home, or take it to one of the local Chinese emporiums and ask them to produce brown-gravy spareribs. As it is, we'll have to go up to Portland again sometime.

It's been said that when Nisei meet each other for the first time, sooner or later they ask, "By the way, what camp were you in?" Because being locked up in an American concentration camp was an almost universal experience for Japanese Americans on the mainland, it is understandable that the question should be raised.

Now that Nisei as a generation are well into their sunset years, another routine question has taken on significance. When you inquire about a Nisei friend's health, it's out of genuine concern rather than routine courtesy. On February 4, 1994, I wrote:

> I suppose it would be fair to say Nisei as a group didn't pay much attention to balanced nutrition in their early years. They grew up during the Depression, and later the fare in the camps wasn't ideal. For many, what they ate was less a matter of choice than what was available or affordable. That didn't include much red meat, which is frowned on these days. In any event, their diet was not typically American. It was more likely to be a com-

bination of American and Japanese, a menu that has continued to be followed somewhat through their lifetimes.

Thus I was interested in a booklet titled *Hints From Horizon for Healthy Living,* published by an organization called Nikkei Horizons of Seattle. It provides information about healthy eating in general, but with some eye-opening data about the nutritional value of some Japanese foods. Pauline Shiosaki is the consulting dietitian, and Margaret Yanagimachi, who sent me the booklet, coordinated the project.

Many persons with heart or kidney problems are on low-sodium diets, which, in practice, means low-salt. But 3.5 ounces of umeboshi (pickled plums) contains 6,600 milligrams of sodium; 3.5 ounces of kelp, 3,100 milligrams of sodium; 3.5 ounces of takuwan (pickled giant radish), 2,800 milligrams of sodium; 3.5 ounces of hijiki (a dried seaweed—my dictionary says "spindle-shaped bladder leaf"), 1,500 milligrams.

I do not know why 3.5 ounces is considered a portion. One of these days, I hope to find out why this is so, and how one calculates 3.5 ounces without a pharmacy scale.

By contrast to the above, shrimp and crab (who can afford them?) pack very little sodium but a lot of another no-no, cholesterol. Tofu has almost no sodium or cholesterol and tastes like it unless you douse it with soy sauce, which has a lot of sodium.

When I was a youngster, my mother not infrequently would serve okara, which is the fibrous leftovers from soybeans used in making tofu and looks and tastes like coarse sawdust. The Horizon booklet notes that while bran these days is considered the best and least expensive food to add fiber to the diet, okara is better. So I guess Mom knew what she was doing when she tried to save money by filling us with a tofu by-product.

Okara, which can be dried at home (the booklet tells you how) and kept indefinitely, also is reported to be excellent in baked goods and can be used in place of bread or cracker crumbs.

Once again East meets West. Bon appétit.

Chapter Nine

The "Japanese" in Japanese American

Being an American of Japanese ancestry is somewhat different from being an American of English, German, Italian, or Scandinavian descent. This, in fact, is what *Out of the Frying Pan* is all about. Though racism against Japanese Americans played a prominent role in upholding this distinction, the tendency among many Japanese Americans to cling to Japanese tradition in the face of their rejection by America's majority culture only underscores it. I express neither pride nor resentment in saying this. It's simply a fact. And that fact has led to some interesting experiences and earnest thinking among my contemporaries, which resulted in a number of columns, including the following, published on June 21, 1985.

Some of my colleagues have expressed concern from time to time about the inability of Japanese Americans to establish their identity in this, their native land. It is a real and not always pleasant concern.

Even a century after Japanese immigrants began to arrive in the United States, the descendants unto the third and fourth generations continue to be regarded as outlanders by a distressing number of their fellow citizens. They are victims of a stereotype that says anyone with oriental features is a fresh-off-the-boat newcomer not quite deserving of acceptance as an American, never mind what history says.

You might call this anti-orientalism. But it's probably more accurate to blame ignorance based on insensitivity rather than malice. Some people refer to Japanese as "Japs" without meaning to be offensive, without understanding the bitter history that makes the word so demeaning.

How do you fight ignorance? By education. As when Congressman Norman Mineta chides Interior Secretary Don Hodel for a Department of the Interior press release describing the Manzanar WRA camp as having been "established for protection against espionage and sabotage." Misconceptions, like noxious weeds, are hardy things, and it will take constant vigilance to prevent them from being revived and repeated.

Sitting around chewing the fat the other day, some of us wondered aloud whether our emphasis on ethnic cultures—a laudable movement in itself—isn't responsible in part for the difficulty that Japanese Americans have in establishing their identity as unadulterated Americans. What follows is a digest of some of the thoughts we kicked around without arriving at a conclusion.

We are told that we should have pride in our Japanese origins, and we do. We are told that Japanese culture is splendid and has much to contribute to the potpourri of America, and we agree. We are told that Japanese American organizations—like the Japanese American Citizens League—are necessary, and we support them.

But in the face of the reality that we are racially distinguishable from the American majority, does our continuing emphasis on the Japanese part of the Japanese American milieu enhance misconceptions about what we really are?

If this is so, and—aside from the justice or injustice of it all—if we are truly concerned about establishing our identity, is there merit in returning to long-ago grade school maxims that taught us to forget the old-country culture and strive to be 110 percent Americans?

What our teachers taught the Nisei in ghetto schools flies in the face of current teaching that we are a pluralistic society and our many cultural backgrounds should be blended into a strong and interesting nation. But the reality is that for some the blending doesn't work, in our case because the majority overlooks the "American" part of "Japanese American" when we ourselves emphasize the "Japanese."

That being the case, does something else need to be tried? Our fat-chewing colleagues were unable to reach a consensus, mostly because we, as the Americans that we are, aren't given to agreeing on much of anything.

The experience of being stereotyped because of race led to two columns, one of which appeared on January 19, 1996.

Near the end of a long, wearisome flight recently, I fell into an exhausted sleep. The next thing I knew, someone was tapping me on the shoulder. It was the stewardess, a middle-aged motherly sort that, because of seniority rules, one sees frequently on overseas routes these days.

"Would you like some coffee or orange juice before we land?" she asked.

Still befuddled by sleep, I looked at her blankly. She spoke to me again, this time slowly, enunciating each word with exaggerated clarity:

"Would . . . you . . . like . . . some . . . cof-fee . . . or . . . or-ange . . . juice . . . be-fore . . . we . . . land?"

Then it hit me. She thought I was Japanese. There were several Japanese on the plane, and she thought I was one of them. She thought I didn't understand English, and she was trying to be kind, trying to help me comprehend what she was saying.

"Yes," I replied. "Yes, I'd like some coffee."

Thinking about it later, I wondered if I should have said, "Hell yes, Sis, gimme a cup of java, no cream." That way, there would be no doubt about my nationality.

On another occasion not long ago, I went to a luncheon hosted by a Japanese group in a downtown Denver hotel frequently used by Japanese. There was an attractive little blonde girl waiting to escort guests into the room. As I approached, she smiled prettily and bowed graciously in welcome.

That took me aback. You don't expect that from an American girl in an American hotel. I responded with a slight bow, the way a Japanese businessman would do, and smiled at her the way a Japanese businessman would not do.

Later, I wondered if I had acted correctly. Should I have said, "Look, miss, this is America, and I'm an American and you're an American, and I don't think there's anything in your hotel employees' manual that says you have to act Japanese just because a guest looks like he might be Japanese."

Or was I right in what I did, which was to let her assume that just because someone looks Japanese, he certainly must be Japanese and should be treated like a Japanese.

That, of course, perpetuates the stereotype that one has to be white or black to be American, and all people with Asian faces are Asians. That is the kind of thinking that persists, even though people like Lance Ito, the judge in the O.J. Simpson trial, to cite a recent high-profile example, demonstrated for all the country that Americans come in a variety of sizes, shapes, colors, and ethnic backgrounds. And they don't have to be bowed to.

Would it have been more proper to stop to chat with her and, in a courteous and kindly manner, let her find out without hurting her feelings that not everyone is what he or she might appear to be?

I was surprised a few days later to receive a letter from a white American in Oakland, California, requesting anonymity and taking me to task for the column. "Rather than taking umbrage as you have done, you might well have written in a manner that reflected bemusement over the situation," he wrote. He continued.

"White America does not have a monopoly on racist attitudes. The various Asian communities here in the U.S. of A. have their own ways of expressing their racism, and only someone who refuses to see the truth would deny it. Or is it your premise that only white bigotry is to be talked about and all the rest ignored?"

I had never been accused of reverse bigotry, and I thought that I had written in a "bemused" manner without "taking umbrage," but if what I was writing was seen in that light, I realized I needed to be more careful.

The other column on mistaken identities was written on November 8, 1991 and follows:

Even if Japanese Americans wanted to forget about what is called the Evacuation, with a capital E, which doesn't seem likely, the American public isn't ready to let them.

There still are many people who don't know about this episode of history, are horrified when they get an inkling of what happened, and want to learn about it. Still others know a little and have a morbid fascination about hearing more. In these precincts, hardly a month goes by without someone calling for a speaker. It is not always easy to find one. There are other things to do.

A library in a local suburb scheduled a speaker one recent day, and I would like to tell you about an interesting sidelight. The sponsors titled the presentation "A Mistake of Terrifically Horrible Proportions," which would indicate a sympathetic viewpoint.

A neatly printed flier with appropriate text was prepared to publicize the event. And then, to make the flier more attractive, someone at the library sought out a Japanese woman and asked her to take brush in hand and produce some appropriate kanji calligraphy.

She brushed two characters that, I am told, together mean *machigai,* which means "mistake" or "error." I do not know whether she chose the word or it was suggested to her, but that is not important. The characters were reproduced in bright red ink and took up about half the space on the flier. The effect was startling, which, of course, was the objective.

But it didn't occur to anyone involved that the whole story of the Evacuation was distorted by illustrating the flier, fifty years after the event, with Japanese characters.

Why?

More than two-thirds of the imprisoned were not Japanese, but Americans. By far the greatest number of victims of the

outrage, the injustice, were Americans, and to indicate they were
Japanese by using Japanese characters to refer to them was to
extend the error.

Would anyone think of using Spanish to decorate a poster
promoting a talk by Federico Peña, Denver's Hispanic ex-mayor?
Of course not. Would anyone come up with Gaelic lettering to
publicize an appearance by Senator Ted Kennedy? Be sensible.
Why, then, is it simply natural, almost obligatory, to link kanji
to Americans of Japanese origins?

Kanji undoubtedly looked like a good idea, and that's more
disturbing than the fact that the characters were used. We were
regarded as "Japanese" rather than Americans in 1942. That
was the public's mindset. That's what enabled the authorities to
get away with referring to citizen Nisei as "non-aliens" in the
documents that authorized our confinement, and the public to
accept the outrage.

Now, a half century later, in the public eye, we are still linked
with a kind of writing that few of us understand and none of us
uses. In its place, the linkage to Japan and Japanese culture is
quite proper, but not in this context. Something is wrong with
the way we are identifying ourselves, and it needs to be corrected.

The emphasis on "Japanese-ness," or perhaps the ability of some of
us to slip easily from one culture to another, was the subject of a column
on October 16, 1992.

This is partly about a woman whom we shall call Daizie. It is
not her real name, but that is not important. Daizie was born
and reared in Japan, married an American, and moved to this
country many years ago. Languages are not one of Daizie's
strong points. Even after long residence in the United States,
her English leaves much to be desired.

Daizie has a number of Nisei friends. A half dozen Nisei were
sitting around at a party, chattering among themselves in English, which, of course, is their native tongue. Nothing unusual
about that. Then Daizie wandered over and joined the group.

Abruptly, everyone shifted linguistic gears, and, smooth and natural as you please, the conversation continued in Japanese without a hitch.

Nobody suggested they speak in Japanese to accommodate Daizie. They just did, automatically, without any kind of signal, and no one thought anything of it.

It struck me that there was something unusual here. A half dozen people thinking nothing of switching away from their native language in their native country to speak a foreign one because one person was uncomfortable with English.

Why did this happen? Was Daizie so helpless that she had to be catered to in this way even after so many years? Was it a compassionate move, begun when Daizie was new to America, and continued without further thought? Or, on the other hand, was she such a domineering figure that she could bend the others to her will, that her friends, without thinking, felt compelled to do what was pleasant for her?

The oddity was that Daizie, despite her problems, is able to express herself better in English than some of the others could speak in Japanese. Yet Japanese was the tongue of choice whenever she joined a group.

Although Daizie is not directly involved, I've witnessed something of the same sort among Nisei in the observance of old-country customs. When associating with a Japanese family, we do things a certain way because it is their custom, even though this is the U.S. of A. Why is it not proper to do things our way and let them adjust? Why do we have to bow just because they do? Isn't a handshake good enough? Why can't we do it our way and let them wrestle with the propriety of helping a lady with her chair at the dinner table?

I don't know the answers. I'm just wondering about why we do the strange things we do. Or maybe they really aren't strange.

One aspect of Japanese culture visible in Japanese Americans is their reluctance to complain even when justified. Their instinct is to avoid confrontation. I addressed that matter in a column published on May 19, 1989.

> You board an airliner, find your place, and discover the space under the seat in front of you is taken up by a large pair of shoes belonging to the fellow sitting there. That space is yours. That's where you are supposed to put your feet and whatever you brought aboard that doesn't fit into the overhead bin. What should you do about reclaiming your space? Which of the following would you choose?
>
>> (a) Tap the guy on the shoulder and say, "Hey, buddy, your gunboats are in the way. Put them somewhere else."
>> (b) Tap the guy on the shoulder and say, "Excuse me. Your shoes are in my way. Would you mind moving them?"
>> (c) Say loudly, "Who in the hell belongs to these shoes?" and kick them into the aisle.
>> (d) Remain silent but sneakily kick the shoes out of the way.
>> (e) Ask the stewardess to do something about your problem.
>> (f) Sulk.
>> (g) Ask the stewardess for a cup of coffee and pour the coffee into the guy's shoes.
>
> A Japanese freelance writer named Shun Daichi had precisely this problem with someone else's shoes. He wrote about it in the newspaper *Jitsugyo no Nihon,* and I happened to see a translation. I found the article remarkable because Daichi brought a racial angle into his essay.
>
> Daichi wrote that the man in front was a "heavy-set Caucasian." Instead of talking to him directly, Daichi asked the stewardess, a Chinese, to do something. She said she could do nothing. Daichi says he angrily thought to himself, "This little Chinese woman is scared of that big white man, so she is letting him get away with it."
>
> Daichi says he seethed for about ten minutes before he calmed down enough to ask the man, politely but firmly, to move his shoes. Daichi writes, "The man bent down and reluctantly moved his shoes. He did it haughtily and without an apology. Before

long, his shoes drifted back to my feet. This time I kicked them forward. After that, they didn't invade my territory again."

I find it interesting that a Japanese could make such a big thing out of what, to Americans, would be a routine matter, and that makes for an interesting psychological study. Daichi writes:

"I think Japanese have trouble airing grievances with foreigners, particularly Caucasians. When we do complain, we usually wind up sounding awkward or even rude. The language barrier, of course, is a large part of the problem. But we also tend to be defensive and negative about ourselves."

I think he's right, and more's the pity.

Getting back to the quiz I devised above, I would guess that most Japanese Americans would go for b, d, and finally e. We are accustomed to coping with rudeness, but at the same time, we retain a certain civility. Why? To avoid confrontation—which may be a cultural trait—or, to put it another way, to not risk a punch in the nose. What do you think?

I addressed this matter in another column, which appeared on June 21, 1996. (That spareribs were involved is an unimportant coincidence; we do not order ribs every time we eat out.)

Not long ago, we went out to satisfy a hankering for barbecued ribs, the kind where a whole slab of what's called "baby backs" is served with a coating of spicy sauce. There isn't a whole lot of meat on the ribs, but what there is is chewy and dripping with flavor.

Well, as sometimes happens, the ribs placed in front of us were not as good as they should have been. They were dry, as though they had been cooked the previous day and simply warmed up prior to serving.

On the other hand, they weren't terribly bad, either. So, grumbling just a little, we started on them. But the deeper we got into the ribs, the more evident it became that they were not up to standard. We should have stopped eating and complained to the waiter. But the waiter had disappeared, and before we knew it, we had finished the ribs.

Eventually, the waiter came with the check. "And how was your dinner?" he asked. That's what they always ask.

Should I have just said the meal was okay and let it go at that?

Or, notwithstanding the bare bones on the plate, should I have told him honestly that the ribs were dry and disappointing?

Well, that's what I did. I told him the ribs were dry and I had been disappointed.

The waiter could have pointed out the bare bones and asked truculently why I hadn't complained before I ate the whole thing. But he didn't. Perhaps wondering about the tip, he said he was sorry and added that if I had brought the problem to his attention earlier, he would have been happy to replace the order. He also asked whether I wanted him to ask the manager to cancel the bill.

That was a clever tactic that put me on the defensive. I said no, I'd eaten the meal, so I would pay for it.

I am no longer young. In our society, age gives a person the prerogative to be outspoken regardless of whether he is listened to. Decades ago, when I was half my present age, would I have had the gumption in a similar circumstance to complain to the waiter? Or, playing the part of the reluctant Asian, would I simply have kept my mouth shut?

To be honest, I think I would not have complained. I have changed with age and the influence of our outspoken times, and now I rather enjoy speaking what's left of my mind.

And what about today's young Japanese Americans? Certainly they are more outspoken than their parents and grandparents were, but do they still retain some of that traditional reluctance to speak out that the eminent sociologist, Dr. Harry Kitano, described as the *enryo* syndrome. I don't know. Maybe, if I promise not to complain, you'd like to think about it and explain it to me.

When the incident of the dry ribs took place, the thought that I might be insulted for complaining never entered my mind. A half century ago, when I was less self-assured and more shy about asserting myself, it might have. An earlier restaurant experience had led to another column about cultural differences that affect the way we react to bumps in the road of life. It was published on May 4, 1990.

At a local restaurant the other day, we noticed that the fork set out on the table with knife and spoon had a bit of the previous user's lunch still stuck on the tines. That's not a sight to stimulate appetites or respect for the establishment, but it seems to happen not infrequently.

The next time the waitress swished by, I held up the fork without a word.

"Oh," she exclaimed. "You got something extra." Without another word, she took the fork away and brought another one. No apology. No expressions of embarrassment. End of incident, to be regarded casually as though it were a routine happening, which probably it was.

You know how an incident like this would be treated in a restaurant in Japan? The waitress would be mortified, there would be a lot of bowing and a string of apologies. And chances are the manager would come over to extend his regrets that the honored guest had been offended.

If the Japanese apology is overly profuse, it hardly gives the impression of lacking sincerity. Chances are they're really, truly sorry they goofed. (Of course, this wouldn't happen in a Japanese-style restaurant that provides pristine, previously unused chopsticks.)

On the other hand, the casual attitude of the American waitress, which we've come to expect and tolerate, would be highly offensive to a Japanese tourist. "Insolent woman," he might mutter, "she takes me for a fool." Chances are the attitude, rather than the lack of sanitation, would be the more offensive.

Differences in culture and perceptions between Americans and Japanese can create and have created misunderstandings and bruised feelings. One example from true life has to do with the Japanese teenager who is a guest in an American home. He has been told to consider himself one of the family and help himself to anything he needs.

The day is warm and he becomes thirsty. Instead of going to the refrigerator, as his host expects him to do, he does what he would do at home in Japan. Continuing to lounge in his chair, he says, "Give me coke." Because he is unsure of his English, he says it more loudly than necessary.

But from his point of view, this is a perfectly proper request. He thinks in Japanese that he would like to have a soft drink, so he composes a sentence mentally in Japanese, then translates it into English. The Japanese sentence was a polite *"Coke wo kudasai,"* and its proper translation is "Give me Coke," which he says from the depths of the easy chair.

What he doesn't realize is that what he thought was a polite request comes out as an arrogant demand. He doesn't realize that he should have gone to the refrigerator himself—in his culture it would be proper to wait for a second or third invitation—or said, "May I have a Coke," or "Please give me Coke." In his ignorance, he makes himself appear as a demanding foreigner, and his hosts may repeat the story to their friends, and before long an entire people is being criticized and Japanese students become unwelcome.

It is common for Japanese Americans of my generation to adopt American first names but not tamper with family names. Thus, as I have said earlier, I was named Kumpei Hosokawa at birth but became William Hosokawa. Then Bill Hosokawa.

Common folks in Japan did not have surnames until 1875. Surnames were reserved for important people, like samurai and warlords, and a few who were given the privilege as a reward for some meritorious action. Take the case of Manjiro, the castaway fisherman who was rescued by an American whaling ship in 1841, got an American education, and returned to Japan with knowledge about the West. He was granted a family name, Nakahama, and that was a great honor. But by 1870, the leaders of the new Japan realized the impracticality of the masses having only first names and eventually decreed that everyone should have a surname.

The three most common Japanese surnames are said to be Sato, Suzuki, and Takahashi. Sato, I am told, derives from the famed Sato clan of warlords and, for some reason unfathomable to most Japanese as well as Westerners, is written with two Chinese characters meaning "to rescue" and "wisteria." Suzuki can be translated as "bell tree," and Takahashi is "high bridge." Hosokawa is written with characters meaning "thin" or "narrow" and "river," which would translate to "brook." The name was relatively unknown in the United States until a Hosokawa, scion of a family that descended from feudal warlords, was named prime minister several years ago. He did not last long, but he succeeded in getting many of my acquaintances to ask me if we were related. The answer is no, he is an aristocrat, and my grandfather was a proud peasant.

Be that as it may, some Japanese names cause a problem for English-speakers, and mine was no exception. That led to the following column on February 25, 1994.

In our part of town is a restaurant that specializes in hamburgers. Big, juicy hamburgers loaded with cholesterol. We go there frequently.

The procedure is that we place our order and pay for it at a counter, give our first name and initial of the last name, and then go find a table. When the order is ready, an attendant picks up a microphone and calls the customer's name—Bill H in my case—and we go up to claim the food.

There may be other Bill H's in the neighborhood, but never have we ordered hamburgers at the same moment. At least, there has been no confusion. Neither has my last name been horribly mangled, as has been the case in a few other restaurants, where it has been necessary to get on the hostess's wait list. Most of them do pretty well with unfamiliar names, but there is little comfort when they screw up.

I suppose I shouldn't feel that way. On the other hand, a person's name is his or her property, and he or she is entitled to have it treated properly, even if it is Bugdanowitz, Ghadaifchian, or Dung rather than Jones or Smith. I am not making up these names. Bob Bugdanowitz was an attorney I used to know, and the others I found in the phone directory.

(I used to know a fellow in Seattle named Ichiro—shortened to Ichi by his Nisei friends. His last name was pronounced "noh-se" but spelled Nose, and that was the cause for some snickers. And my friend Toshio Hoshide, now deceased, in Washington D.C. has been called Mr. Hoss Hide on occasion.)

But I digress. What I started out to do was to discuss the propriety, the next time we go out to dine rather than simply to eat, of giving my name to the hostess as Bill H. Would she be comfortable in announcing to the waiting multitude that H's table is ready? Would I be more comfortable being summoned to dinner as Bill H than as Mr. Hoe-sok-wah, with the emphasis on "sok"?

Should I choose to be listed as Bill H, it is predictable that I would be chided by contemporaries who would call it a cowardly denial of Asian heritage. They would argue that I should take pride in my name and use any mispronunciation as an opportunity to correct and educate the ignorant.

And presumably there would be others who would counsel pragmatism—what the heck, be practical rather than needlessly idealistic and do what's comfortable.

Actually, this isn't an overwhelming problem. Our occasions for dining out are outnumbered by excursions to the Bill H–type places. And it doesn't bother me a great deal if infrequently the name is mangled. Hosokawa doesn't seem to be particularly difficult, especially since the prime minister of Japan has been mentioned frequently on television.

Good old Bob Bugdanowitz has gone to his reward, but if I should ever encounter Mr. Ghadaifchian or Mr. Dung, I must remember to ask how they feel about their perfectly good family names in an English-speaking society.

If Americans have difficulty with Japanese words, and they do, Japanese have equal difficulty with English. As their culture changes, Japanese young people have adopted many Western concepts—and the words to describe them—with sometimes startling results. Here are some, reported in the column for May 11, 1990.

Broadly speaking, the Japanese have a difficult time with spoken English. But they have an amazing knack for adapting English words and phrases into expressions that, while they may not be true to original meanings, fit their contemporary lifestyle.

One well-known example is the word *mansion,* which in English means an opulent house. In Japan a *manshon* is an apartment just a notch more luxurious than an *apahto,* which is a dinky little unit in an apartment building.

(My friend Lee Chia recalls being asked the difference between a Tokyo *manshon* and an *apahto.* His reply: "In a *manshon,* one does not hang laundry out the window to dry.")

A recent article in the *Japan Times* of Tokyo by Katsuaki Horiuchi, professor of English literature at Meiji University, provides some amusing insights into the way with-it young Japanese have developed a trendy vocabulary by adapting English words. Some of the new words have only a tenuous tie to the original meaning, but they can be fun. Here are some of Horiuchi's examples.

Abauto-na: From "about." It means to be random or irresponsible.

Ribasu-suru: To do "reverse." Means to throw up.

Chekku-suru: To check. Means to look over someone of the opposite sex.

Makku, or *Makkudo:* From "McDonalds," whose hamburgers are enjoying a booming prosperity.

Kenta: From "Kentucky Fried Chicken," of course.

Amekaji: Shortened form of "American casual," as in clothing.

Itakaji: Shortened form of "Italian casual."

Guddo desu yo: "It's good," used in reference to freedom, comfort, and style in a person or thing.

Gyaru, which is about as close as most Japanese tongues can come to "girl" or "gal." *Oyaji-gyaru* (daddy girl) refers to young women who do things their fathers do, such as play golf, dabble in the stock market, drink in pubs, and gamble. They are *bode-kon,* or body-conscious, like to *asashan* (shampoo their hair in the morning), are likely to be *bairin-gyaru* (bilingual girls). And women (seemingly better at foreign tongues than their male contemporaries) who speak three languages are, of course, *trairin-gyaru.*

JAR, pronounced "jaru," not to be confused with JAL (Japan Air Lines), which also comes out of Japanese mouths as "jaru," is another new word heard frequently in certain circles. The JAR "jaru" refers to three Christian colleges, *Jochi* (Sophia), *Aoyama Gakuin*, and *Rikkyo*, attended by many fashionable young women from well-to-do families.

And then there's *sekuharu,* which, understandable in these times, comes from "sexual harassment."

Observes Horiuchi: Creating trendy words is a way of having fun with words, but they are also a mirror of the society that creates them.

Ah, me, what might my father, who left struggling Meiji Era Japan in 1899, say about the lexicon of the new, hip, with-it language if he were alive to experience it?

And in a somewhat similar vein on June 16, 1989:

Probably it was back in the uncomplicated, innocent days when "knock-knock" was the rage. Remember them?

You'd say, "Knock-knock," and your friend asks, "Who's there?"

Then you'd say something like "Sam and Janet."

"Sam and Janet who?" And your response would be:

"Sam and Janet Evening," even humming a bit, and if your friend didn't get it, you'd laugh like crazy.

And here's another one.

"Knock-knock."

"Who's there?"

"Asia."

"Asia who?"

"Asia gonna ask me in?"

Well, anyway, I seem to recall that contemporaneous with "Knock-knock" was "Confucius Say." All sorts of pseudo-wise sayings—"Confucius say only damn fool spit against high wind"—were attributed to the ancient Chinese philosopher. These days you might find this sort of thing demeaning, but back then it was just another diversion, without hint of racism.

If you look it up in your encyclopedia, you'll find that Confucius lived 551–479 b.c., when moral and cultural traditions were in serious decline. Perhaps our times are somewhat comparable. Confucius gathered hundreds of students around him and offered education and moral teachings to any who would come. He taught the value of learning, honesty in social relations, respect for one's parents and family, the nobility of hard work, and the importance of harmony in all dealings.

Some of his teachings were collected in the Analects of Confucius, which were spread across Asia with the advance of Chinese culture. Confucianism has played a large part in the moral and philosophical teachings that are part of the upbringing of Chinese, Koreans, Vietnamese, and Japanese, among others.

Some observers, noting the exceptionally high scholastic records of Asian Americans in U.S. schools, have suggested that the Confucian respect for education and family solidarity may have more than a little to do with it. Although I am not aware of any scholarly study into this theory, it seems plausible.

On a recent visit to Taiwan, the conversation with an educator got around to the generally deplorable state of high school education in the States, the high drop-out rate, the staggering number of functionally illiterate adults. I asked whether he thought a good shot of Confucian values would be of benefit to Americans.

He gave me a thoughtful look and then replied: "Well, we haven't succeeded in launching a satellite yet."

I think it was meant to be a roundabout compliment, or perhaps a disclaimer. Unfortunately, the conversation went on to other things before I could tell him I was a literal-minded American unaccustomed to indirection and ask him to explain. Ever since, I have been wondering what he really meant. I would like to think he was urging me not to despair for America, but I'm not at all sure.

Chapter Ten
Myths and Truths

Mike Royko, the late syndicated newspaper columnist, was marvelous at satirical humor. One day he wrote about the poor in America. His column was based on some findings by the Heritage Foundation, which is a think tank that leans somewhat to the right of center and therefore is disliked by those who lean to the left. Royko's column inspired me to write the following, published November 1, 1991:

> According to Mike Royko, the Census Bureau determined that there are about thirty million "poor" in the United States, and the Heritage Foundation found that 38% of them own their own homes, the median value being $39,000. While $39,000 doesn't buy much in the way of shelter these days, the homes are presumed to have a roof, heating, and running water. And half are reported to have air-conditioning.

> Further, Royko reports, Heritage Foundation's survey found 62% of "poor" households own cars, and 14% have more than one. What's even more impressive, 31% own microwave ovens. He made no mention of TV ownership, but I would think they are a necessity of life in most households.

> What this adds up to is that motor vehicles, air-conditioning in our homes, and a variety of electric and electronic gadgets

are owned, in our civilization, even by those classified as "poor." Somehow, it seems, there is a need for a new definition of *poor* and *poverty.*

Go back with me now to the autumn of 1942. Across the interior of the nation, the rude, army-type barracks in ten jerry-built detention camps had been filled with evacuees from the West Coast. And in areas around the camps, farmers and townspeople who had opposed the influx of these people suddenly saw in them a source of labor to help harvest sugar beets that otherwise would be lost.

Cynically calling on the patriotism of the imprisoned, they urged the evacuees to volunteer for farm labor. Some 10,000 men left the camps and saved the crop to help refill the nation's sugar bowls and save the economy of countless dusty towns.

There was an interesting sidelight. Many of the evacuees left the camps to get away from the primitive conditions that existed behind the barbed wire. What they found on the farms of the Intermountain West, which depended heavily on migrant labor at peak periods, was even more primitive conditions. At least the camps had electricity, running water, and showers that were hot most of the time.

When the evacuee laborers complained, employers were outraged. Who were these "Japs" to grumble about conditions that were good enough for the farmers themselves, let alone itinerant migrant field hands?

It was a weird situation: Japanese American farmers who had been criticized for living under substandard conditions on the West Coast (and accused of holding down the American standard of living), locked up in rude prison camps, then being asked as a patriotic duty to work and live under even more disgraceful conditions.

Looking back on those times today, contemplating the current definition of poverty, it is hard to decide whether to laugh or cry.

Academics and specialists understand that all Asians are not alike, but much of the American public and the newspapers that serve them still don't, as the following column, published on May 27, 1994, suggests.

The press recently reported findings by UCLA's Professor Paul Ong that there's a lot of poverty among Asian Pacific Americans. Ong found that while many are economically successful, many others (mainly Vietnamese, Cambodians, and Laotians) are impoverished and depend heavily on welfare. The headline over the story in one newspaper declared: "Study says Asian affluence a myth."

Unfortunately, in the public mind all Asians are lumped together as one people. In reality, there is as much difference among various Asian groups as there is among the people of Europe. We are aware of the difference between Swedes and Bosnians, for example, or Germans and French. Yet we don't understand that Japanese are different from Malays, who are different from Koreans, who are different from Thais in culture, history, language, etc.

Aside from these differences, the time they've had to adapt to American civilization varies widely. Some Chinese Americans can trace their ancestry to the men who helped build the transcontinental railroad soon after the Civil War. Some Japanese Americans are of the fourth and fifth generations of their families in the U.S. And some, like the Southeast Asians who fled the Communists in Indochina, have been here less than a decade.

Inevitably, the newest of the newcomers start at the bottom of the economic ladder, working long hours at low-paying jobs while they scratch out a handhold, learning the language and the customs and saving a few bucks to invest. At this stage of their history in the United States, many no doubt are impoverished, but chances are they won't stay that way. Some may be washing dishes or waiting tables today in a Chinese restaurant, but you can bet that many of them will be running their own places before long.

Members of a Korean immigrant family might start as hired hands in a cheap motel, working and saving until eventually they can buy the place and go into business for themselves, run a grocery store on the side, and make enough money to send their kids to college. The grandparents of affluent Japanese American professionals—doctors, lawyers, scientists, business executives—probably started as railroad section hands and moved in time to farming or small business.

That's the way it was, and is, with all immigrant groups. Yet many Americans express surprise that the descendants of long-ago immigrants from Asia today are "affluent," and that the most recent immigrants from Asia are having a tough time. Why? Because they see all Asians not as individuals or of different ethnic groups, but as a single people with a single history. The stereotype of the inscrutable Oriental dies hard.

One of these days, I suppose, our country will quit seeing stereotypes, be they Asians or whatever, and understand that all of us are individuals significantly different from each other.

The subject of diversity among Asian Americans as well as among Japanese Americans must have weighed on my mind. On October 6, 1995, I wrote:

What, the reporter asked, is the Japanese American position on this particular issue? What do you folks think about it?

Bum questions. It doesn't really matter what issue the reporter was asking about, because there is no single Japanese American position on anything, except that maybe rice is better than potatoes at dinnertime. The questions are irrelevant. We are as diverse in our opinions and interests and activities as the rest of America.

Witness the ongoing investigation into the tragic Ruby Ridge shoot-out in Idaho in 1992. An FBI task force attacked the isolated mountain cabin of Randy Weaver, identified as a government-hating, ultrarightist extremist, and killed his wife and son. One of the eleven FBI sharpshooters carrying out orders to shoot was a ten-year veteran of the agency named Lon Horiuchi, a Japanese name.

Witness the founder of the National Commodity and Barter Association. He calls himself one of the leaders of the "freedom movement" and makes his living by helping others avoid paying federal income tax, which he declares is unconstitutional and illegal. He lives in Longmont, Colorado, and his name is Denny Hashimoto.

Witness the president-elect of the elite and conservative 50,000-member University of Washington Alumni Association. His name is Larry Matsuda.

Witness that after more than a half century, some Japanese Americans who were convicted of violating Selective Service laws in World War II are getting some support for their demands for apology from Japanese Americans who criticized them fifty-odd years ago.

Witness the Japanese American National Museum's "National Salute to Japanese American Veterans" in November. The event will commemorate the very substantial contributions of Japanese Americans in the nation's war. Do the veterans have support? Sponsors of the salute expect a sellout crowd of 8,000 for the show following a dinner for 3,000. The event kicks off a museum exhibit called "Fighting for Tomorrow: Japanese Americans in America's Wars."

Witness that some members of the venerable Japanese American Citizens League sought, and got, organizational endorsement for legalization of same-sex marriages. Witness that other members protested futilely that their organization had no business taking sides on such an issue.

Witness that some members of JACL want it to be on the cutting edge of social change. Witness that other members want to limit its activities to issues having a direct bearing on Japanese Americans.

Witness the support of Japanese Americans for California governor Pete Wilson's cutback on social assistance for illegal immigrants, and vigorous opposition to that policy from another sector of the community.

Who's right and who's wrong? Well, everybody and nobody. We've come to the stage of just being and acting like the diverse peoples who make up America, and not an ethnic minority with a monolithic position.

As the preceding column tried to explain, the Japanese American community is a complex body of humans with a wide range of experiences and philosophies—in effect a microcosm of the United States itself. This is difficult to understand because of widespread ignorance and misinformation about the community and the individuals who compose it. As a child, I heard this hurtful taunt from other children: "Chin Chin Chinaman, eats rats." I remembered that when I wrote the following column about the kind of innocent misinformation that blocks understanding. It was published on May 15, 1992.

A person I know who has won awards for her TV documentaries told me recently she was thinking of doing a program on Japanese picture brides who came to the U.S. to marry men they had never seen.

Good idea, if a little late. There may be a few of them still living who could tell firsthand stories, but probably not many. She asked whether she could run some ideas and questions by me about Japanese Americans, and I said sure, no problem.

She has been sending me questions ever since. I am horrified by her ignorance. Let me share a sampling.

Was it true, she asked, that the Issei did not return to Japan because they would be killed if they did?

Nonsense. Thousands of young Japanese males came to the United States at the turn of the century, and shortly thereafter; though many stayed, many others went back to Japan without facing execution.

The producer double-checked her sources, and it turned out that either she, or the person who gave her the information, confused twentieth-century immigration with what happened 350 years earlier. In 1636, in an effort to rid feudal Japan of foreign influence, the Tokugawa shogunate forbade Japanese to go abroad and did not allow them to return if they did leave the country. But that changed after Commodore Perry persuaded Japan, under threat of gunfire, to open its doors in 1854.

Another question: Before World War II, passage back and forth to Japan was not uncommon, but the woman who became known as Tokyo Rose was stuck in Japan because the U.S. government refused to give her the papers necessary to return.

Nonsense again. She and many other Japanese Americans were caught in Japan by the outbreak of war because they didn't realize war was about to start.

Question: Why did most Japanese Americans on the East Coast return to Japan just prior to the war, while those who settled on the West Coast didn't? If they were different, in what way were they different?

Simple. Most of the ethnic Japanese on the East Coast in 1941 were residents of Japan who were in the U.S. temporarily with their families as businessmen representing Japanese companies. As business fell off due to war fears, they went home. The ethnic Japanese on the West Coast were immigrants with American-born offspring, permanent residents of the United States who had no reason to go to Japan, since America was home. Somehow, even today, many people don't understand the difference between Japanese businessmen fresh from Tokyo and fourth- and fifth-generation Americans of Japanese origins.

Where is this TV producer getting this kind of information, which is confused at best and totally false at worst? From, she tells me, a university instructor who teaches a course on Japanese immigration!

And finally, a requiem, published May 2, 1993.

My friend Frank (Taba) Fujita died the other day. He was eighty-three years old, and for fifty-seven of them he was married to one woman. Taba was a good man, gentle, kind, hard-working. He loved his wife and his daughter and grandson and great-grandson.

Taba enjoyed cooking, and for a while he ran a restaurant that gained a considerable measure of acclaim. But for much of his life, he worked in retail markets, like many other Nisei of his time. He could hardly be called exceptional. No flags were flown at half staff in his memory, nor were public offices closed in mourning. He was just a very decent human being who was happy with what he was, and for that he will be missed by his friends.

So this column will not be a lament for Taba Fujita alone, but for an entire generation of very ordinary Nisei good guys and gals who are leaving the scene in increasing numbers.

Look in the back pages of *Pacific Citizen* almost any week, and you will find a lengthy list of people who are no longer with us. Most of their names are familiar only to limited circles of friends and associates. Each was an individual, but collectively they make up a generation that experienced and survived common problems and, in large measure, common frustrations while also, as a group, gaining a measure of success.

That commonality is based on their ethnicity, the fact that they are the offspring of Japanese who immigrated to the United States within the span of a few decades early this century in search of fortune, if not fame. The immigrants carried heavy baggage in trying to make their way in a strange and often unfriendly culture. Their Nisei offspring inherited much of that baggage, and sometimes it was a burden.

At the same time, there was much moral, if abstract, treasure in that baggage. Characteristics like diligence and willingness to work and loyalty and perseverance that helped the Nisei generation to overcome their own vicissitudes, which were many.

I have heard some Sansei—not many, to be sure—complain that it was these very characteristics that held back Nisei economic, social, and political assimilation, that they were too conformist and servile and lacked a rebellious spirit. But that is another story, and you can get a lot of argument about that.

What I wish to declare now is that members of the Nisei generation, fast vanishing from the scene, are leaving a heritage that all Americans will find useful. They took some important values of their Issei parents, perhaps not consciously in all cases, and applied them nonetheless to make a success of their own lives.

I find that admirable. What more can one wish of a people? So let this be a tribute to all the men and women of Taba Fujita's generation whose names appear in the obituaries, and a celebration of the time they spent with us, regardless of what they accomplished in their allotted years. It would be a shame if more about them were not recorded for posterity before all are gone.

Chapter Eleven

In Closing

Well, Bill Hosokawa, you've used up a lot of words telling us what you as a Japanese American think, and what other Japanese Americans ought to think. But do we really know you and what you stand for?
Good question.

In December 1993, Gwen Muranaka, assistant editor of *Pacific Citizen,* interviewed me. Excerpts from that conversation may answer the question.

GWEN: As a journalist reporting on the past and present, what do you think of the Japanese American Citizens League (JACL) as it relates to society and government today? Are we tuned in, are we effective, are we being listened to? Basically, where are we?

HOSOKAWA: The situation has changed drastically since 1935 when I first became interested in JACL. Back in those days a Nisei had very little access to the power structure. You couldn't just go in the mayor's office and say, "This is what we have in mind, and we'd like to have you do it." It's not likely we could have got into his office. Today, we are much more sophisticated, we have more clout, we have Nisei and Sansei in political office, we have members of Congress. We know how to work the establishment. We have people who have access to business and corporate leaders, and they know who we are. And that was a natural development over a period of 50 or 60 years. Back in the 1930s, the average age of a Nisei was about 15 years. There were only a few mature Nisei. Most of them were so busy just trying to establish themselves as individuals in business that we had no real presence in the broader American community. We were pretty much stuck in our Little Tokyo communities.

GWEN: What was the Nisei vision, and do you think it was appropriate for its times? I'm talking of the '30s and '40s.

HOSOKAWA: There wasn't much vision. Mostly, they were struggling to survive. It's been said that in those days more Nisei wearing Phi Beta Kappa keys were stacking oranges in the markets of Los Angeles than there were in white collar jobs. Whatever vision we had was that of equality of opportunity. The Nisei back in the '30s had two strikes against them, one was the racial discrimination they faced. Nisei were being discouraged, as I was, by college professors from studying in certain fields because they said it was a waste of time. The second barrier was that we were in the middle of a terrible economic depression. Our vision was first to survive, second to win a measure of opportunity where we could show we could get the job done. And that situation was responsible in large part for individual entrepreneurship of Nisei who were wise enough not to look for jobs in big business but tried to stand on their own two feet.

GWEN: After Redress, has the leadership today articulated its own vision?

HOSOKAWA: Our leadership today is interested in the problems of all minorities, rather than just Japanese Americans.

GWEN: Good or bad?

HOSOKAWA: Both. It's good to the extent that we have broadened our horizons. We're more concerned about the problems of all minorities, and we want to make this a better America for all Americans. At the same time it is not the kind of pitch that excites many Japanese Americans who have "made it," who are more concerned with their own personal problems and personal advancement. And while the ideal is certainly a noble one, the practical effect on strengthening JACL is a negative one.

GWEN: You have written much about the Issei and Nisei generations with humor, warmth and insight. You have written that the Sansei, the 30–50 age group, is here. What advice would you give to those who are making their way in business, leadership and government?

HOSOKAWA: Giving young people advice is really presumptuous, but let me take a crack at it. I think there is a need for more concern with community affairs, with the problems of all minorities, as well as taking a more active role in the broad community. To become involved in local and national political matters, taking a more active role in local organizations like the library board or the art museum, and not just confine themselves to Japanese American community affairs.

GWEN: Has JACL been pro-active enough? Have we reacted more to crises and problems, rather than having a game plan? Have events shaped the image of the organization or has the organization been able to shape events in relation to its own goals for the Japanese American community?

HOSOKAWA: That is a very complex question. Post-war JACL set its own agenda at the convention in Denver in 1946 when it announced 15 different goals, and among them was redress for the wrongs against them in World War II. It was an inward-looking organization at that time because its problems were our own community problems. They also affected the nation as a whole. For example, the successful effort to eliminate race as a qualification for naturalization helped eliminate racial discrimination on many different levels. And while that goal affected the broad American community, we set that goal primarily because it affected our own community. This was a case where in trying to improve our own situation, we did have an effect on a national shortcoming.

Have the events shaped the image of the organization or has the organization been able to shape events? The answer to that would be, both. As a minority organization we have an agenda to improve our situation. But having made a great deal of progress overcoming problems that affect us directly, we have had to broaden our goals so that we have become interested in the entire Asian Pacific community.

GWEN: As editor of the editorial pages of the *Denver Post* you have been close to politics on all levels. How can Asian Americans get more involved in the political process? How can we gain voice?

HOSOKAWA: As individuals we can get acquainted with local political leadership. We can take part in Republican or Democratic affairs, we can put pressure on individual members of the city council or county commission. That is the most effective way to get action. In Colorado, Adams County is the home of Bob Sakata, a very prominent farmer, and he can pick up the phone at any time and call any of the leaders in his county and say, "This is Bob Sakata and this is what I think." He has a great deal of clout as an individual, not necessarily as a Japanese American. The same could be said in Boulder County where Jim Kanemoto is a powerhouse. He will be listened to as an individual, and not just because he represents Japanese American organizations. He can talk to somebody and say, "This is what I think about this situation." That has more clout than saying, "This is Jim Kanemoto representing the 50 members of the Japanese American community in Longmont." He is talking as a thoughtful member of the community as a whole. That is the way we have to go because we don't have a million voters in the Japanese American community.

GWEN: U.S.-Japan relations are controversial even among members of the JACL. Some feel it is not a worthwhile organizational pursuit. How do you feel?

HOSOKAWA: Even though we are 100 percent Americans, we are affected profoundly by the state of relationships between the U.S. and Japan. The Evacuation is a prime example. Up to fairly recently we may have been reluctant to make our thoughts known, but now I think it is imperative that we speak out. Not because we are pro-Japanese, not because we know a great deal about Japan—most of us know very little about Japan and U.S.-Japan relationships—but if we have feelings about the way things are going or how things should go, I think it is incumbent on us as Americans to speak out. We are now in position to do this without being perceived as apologists for Japan. That means we ought to know of what we speak. We should have a basis for having opinions, and then express those opinions.

GWEN: Culturally speaking, do Japanese Americans still have some difficulty with our identity, our roots, of coming to grips with our heritage?

HOSOKAWA: The identity issue is being put on Japanese Americans by the greater American community. So far as Sansei and Yonsei go, from my observation most have very little concern about Japanese culture and it rarely crosses their minds, though the pressure from the outside makes them aware of it. I have eight grandchildren. Only one of them has any interest in Japanese culture or language.

GWEN: Dr. Harry Kitano says the outmarriage rate of Japanese Americans will become increasingly higher in the years ahead. Do you think this will mean the loss or diffusion of the Japanese culture?

HOSOKAWA: Very definitely it will, although this again is a matter on which it is very difficult to generalize. For example, what happens to a Sansei or Yonsei in Denver would be different from the experience of a Sansei or Yonsei in Los Angeles, where there is a greater number of Japanese Americans, where there is greater contact with the Japanese community.

GWEN: You've written many books from a historical perspective. Are we missing any of the lessons of history?

HOSOKAWA: Yes. The progress that the Nisei and Issei were able to make, in the way of individual and community development, was due in considerable part to the fact that they had to overcome adversity. They had to suffer, and this is an experience alien to later generations. Because of that, interests have been fragmented. The Issei had to work like hell to survive. The Nisei had pressure of all kinds against them, and they had to focus on their individual welfare. The Evacuation was due, in large part, to racial prejudice. And this was something we older Nisei had to cope with. Much of the JACL leadership today has had very little first-hand experience with what the Nisei went through. While the JACL leadership is aware of these problems, the followership, the Sansei and Yonsei, don't spend a lot of time worrying about the pressures of discrimination. That has to be pointed out to them by JACL telling them, "Hey, we have to be concerned about this." But I feel that to most Sansei and Yonsei, what the Nisei see as problems are simply bothersome diversions in a life of trying to improve their economic status, raising kids, trying to get ahead in their jobs. The impact of what some people would see as major problems doesn't really register on the majority of Japanese Americans. And that makes it difficult for an organization like JACL, which needs conflict to thrive.

GWEN: Is JACL leadership missing any significant issues?

HOSOKAWA: Sometimes I get a feeling that we are looking for issues to become indignant about. The issues today pale by comparison to the great issues of the past that affected all of us as a people and the United States itself. How can we get excited, as some Japanese Americans have, about the thrust of a Hollywood potboiler when we have come through the experience of serving time in a concentration camp because our nation was insensitive, unaware of, or careless about how the Bill of Rights was violated? It's an altogether different scale. JACL is, I think, less constructive about meeting the needs of our people than it has been. The effort seems to be reactive. Something happens, then we get mad about it, instead of going about addressing a problem in a constructive manner. I think the word they use is *proactive.* I am concerned that many of our brightest and best people are not involved in JACL. There is a very large number of Japanese Americans who are making a mark in the worlds of business, law, science and government outside of JACL, who get no space in the Japanese American press simply because they are not out there raising hell, complaining about something. In reality, they are making very significant contributions to the economic and social life of the United States as Americans who just happen to be of Japanese descent. I would like to get more of these people involved in the concerns of JACL. They are a great resource that is not being utilized.

GWEN: Resource?

HOSOKAWA: Yes. Just the benefit of their contacts, knowledge and their intelligence. I think JACL has become something of an incestuous organization. We just talk to each other too much. The organization needs new blood.

GWEN: What are your plans for your future?

HOSOKAWA: At my age you don't think very far into the future. But I will continue to work for the University of Denver and the Japan American Society of Colorado. I am interested in U.S.–Japan relations, and I will do whatever I can to improve understanding.

Gwen: Here's an old interview question. When you are gone, what would you like people to say about you? The kind of person you were, your career . . .

Hosokawa: I'd be interested in hearing what they say. (Laughter) . . . I don't know. I think I would be pleased if somebody said, "He cared." Two words.

Over the years, I had been concerned about being excessively militant about our problems, about Japanese Americans being perceived as oversensitive pests and crybabies. Protest strongly against injustice, I urged, insist vigorously for fairness, but don't make a career of looking for matters to complain about. That position was enunciated in columns published as early as October 11, 1968, and as late as June 30, 1997. I give you the most recent one first:

Political cartoonists are an inevitable part of the American way of life. Their job is to be outrageous. Fairness doesn't necessarily have a place in their business. They are paid handsomely to make their subjects squirm and the public laugh, and their tactic is exaggeration. The best seem to dip their pens in vitriol. If your feelings are hurt by a caricature, if you are outraged, there isn't much you can do about it.

No one, particularly a public figure, is immune. The president of the United States, who certainly is entitled to the respect of his office, is a favorite target of cartoonists. Bill Clinton frequently is depicted as a fat slob or as a long-nosed liar like Pinocchio, with an uncomprehending, befuddled look and worse. The First Lady, Hillary Rodham Clinton, has cheeks and teeth that lend themselves to unkind caricature. They may complain privately, but not in public.

The president and Mrs. Clinton and Vice President Al Gore were depicted recently on the cover of *National Review* magazine with what were perceived as buck teeth and slanted eyes, described as "negative Asian features" by an outraged JACL representative. The cover was linked to stories about Asian money supposedly buying political influence. The protest was predictable.

This is not to condone racial stereotyping, but it is illuminating to know that it affects not only Asians but many thoroughly accepted and well-loved ethnic groups. Example: in the San Francisco *Examiner* a couple of years ago, Seattle writer Dominic Gates wrote as follows about popularly celebrated St. Patrick's day:

"You'll see it everywhere on the 17th of March, from Hallmark stores to T-shirts to street banners: a diminutive man with buckles on his shiny shoes and another on his billycock hat, his snub nose, heavy brow and mustacheless beard accentuating a simian quality to his features; he has a pugnacious scowl on his face, his fists are clenched, and he carries a shillelagh."

But all is not fun and good humor. The source of that image, Gates tells us, "is English anti-Irish bigotry from the 19th Century."

How many of us have enjoyed the stereotype of the leprechaun-like Irishman without realizing its bitter origins?

There are other stereotypes, some of which we accept and some we reject. Jews no longer are depicted as big-nosed money-grubbers, probably derived from the Shylock image. But no one seems to object to the Italian portrayal as happy, gregarious people who eat enormous quantities of spaghetti doused with tomato sauce and speak English with an accent. In fact, a food company promoted this image in its advertising and no one seemed upset.

But what would be the reaction of Asian Americans if TV commercials were produced showing a family around the dinner table slurping up instant noodles with chopsticks under the urging of Papa and Mama speaking with a pseudo-oriental accent? Outrage, undoubtedly, and perhaps an organized protest campaign.

Why would happy spaghetti-eaters be looked upon differently from happy noodle-guzzlers? I don't know. Perhaps for the same reason that there is no protest when President Clinton and his wife are portrayed as hogs or liars, but some people become angry when they are caricatured by a political cartoonist with stereotypical Asian features. Incidentally, Japanese cartoonists can be equally savage in caricaturing their politicians, but the

Japanese themselves don't seem to mind.

And here is the earlier column:

One of the speakers in San Diego at a meeting of newspaper editors was Arte Johnson, the little comedian of the highly successful *Laugh-In* TV show who, making like a German soldier in World War II, says, "Verrry eenteresting." For some reason, the public finds it verrry funny. Johnson told us he speaks nothing but English, but he has made a lucrative living with dialect roles. This isn't easy these days because people are so quick to become offended.

Not long ago, Johnson recalled, he pretended on a program to be telling an off-color story in a foreign language. He leered and gestured and laughed lewdly while mouthing a lot of gibberish that he thought sounded the way Polish ought to sound, although he never identified the language he was mimicking. A few days later, he was astonished to receive a letter from some sort of ethnic organization protesting what was described as an unspeakably obscene performance that offended all Polish-speaking Americans.

Johnson wrote back asking for a translation of the story he had told, and predictably he never did get a reply. Johnson told of the incident simply as an anecdote about his experiences, but the moral was only too obvious. Too many folks these days are protesting too much about too many affronts, real and imagined. And when one becomes overly sensitive, a lot of the fun drains out of life, which is a pretty grim business without our purposely making it even more that way.

The next column was included in this collection not because of its profundity or cleverness, but simply because I was moved by the incongruity of the music of Rachmaninoff in a humble noodle shop. It was published November 11, 1989.

Magnificent Heian Shrine is a major attraction in Kyoto, the ancient Japanese capital city replete with tourist attractions. I write today not of the shrine, but of a modest noodle shop a few blocks from Heian's front gate.

The shop is called Kyona-ya, and among a people noted for their love of noodles, Kyona-ya is famed.

Let me tell you how modest the place is. There is seating for nine at the counter, behind which are gas burners for heating the noodles and the delectable soup and the oil for tempura, in addition to a sink for dish washing. Two youngish men who might be brothers cook and serve behind the counter.

In addition there is space for three tiny tables and eight tiny chairs. A woman who might be the wife of one of the men attends these tables and ducks behind the counter to wash the dishes when there is time. Patrons waiting for a seat can take their ease on a hard bench in the shade just outside the front entrance and watch the multicolored taxis—all spotlessly clean—speed by. When a seat opens up, the woman summons you, with gracious apologies for the delay.

Recently, we slurped up noodles at the Kyona-ya's counter, savoring the aromas and flavor of the soup, enjoying the ambiance, and listening to a Rachmaninoff concerto playing softly on the shop's obviously expensive hi-fi system.

If the juxtaposition of an ancient Kyoto Shinto shrine, hot noodle soup in an elbow-to-elbow shop, and a Rachmaninoff tape on hi-fi seemed incongruous, it was the incongruity that marks contemporary Japan.

Here the supermodern world of smart silicon chips and bits and bytes and billion-dollar deals rises out of centuries-old traditions and a culture alien to the Western world.

Japan stubbornly has kept much of the old and embraced the new with astonishing fervor, and made the combination work. The result is not at all unpleasant, as many Americans are discovering.

On a visit to Kyoto several trips back, we noticed a sign that said "Colorado Coffee Shop." Then we saw several more, all over neat little establishments. Hmmm. What was the connection? Had some student who studied in Colorado gone home and opened a chain of shops and named them as an expression of nostalgia?

There had been no opportunity to investigate further until this last visit. After a bowl of noodles, we went for a cup of coffee. This particular Colorado Coffee Shop not only served a pleasantly aromatic beverage, but sold bags of fresh-ground Colorado Blend and Colorado Iced Coffee Blend. But what was the connection to our state, which, unfortunately, grows no coffee?

The manager burst the bubble gently. There is, he said, a Colorado in Brazil, and the Colorado Coffee Shops are a franchised chain that has nothing to do with Norte Americanos. That was one more reminder that the United States of America is not necessarily the center of the universe.

As a finale, I present two columns. One was published January 5, 1968, after I returned to the United States from another of my lengthy reporting trips to the Far East. I had flown all night across the Pacific, and suddenly, there were the golden hills of California.

Our plane dipped low over the San Francisco peninsula, and it was hard to realize this was the homeland. It was easy to let one's imagination run as we floated down toward the airport. That scar across the landscape, marking the route of an advancing thruway, could easily be the raw earth ripped up for a new military airfield in Vietnam. That line of trees—I saw a similar row that sheltered a Vietcong patrol from prying eyes aboard an American helicopter gunship. The mudflats of South San Francisco Bay—from 2,000 feet in the air it might have been the Mekong Delta in flood season.

But the land below us was a land of peace and security, troubled but not despairing. Its people were for the most part clean, well fed, adequately clothed and sheltered. They feared no attack in the night, no midnight raids from police or guerrillas, no terrorist bombs. Food was to be had as close as the nearest supermarket, and one could drink from any tap without fear of dreadful diseases. What a blessed nation is ours.

Each trip abroad is an adventure, but it's always great to come home. And each journey makes this reporter more appreciative, more grateful for America, despite all its obvious shortcomings. We are a nation built on improvement, rising from dissent, but the dissenters and detractors in our midst might think more constructively if they could appreciate what we have in contrast to the rest of the world.

And last, this column from the *Denver Post* in the form of a 1977 Christmas letter to my firstborn son, who was by then a college professor.

Dear Mike,

A long time ago, when you were just a toddler, you were a small part of a dramatic Christmas experience. Of course, you were too young to remember, but it is worth knowing about, so let me tell you the story now.

It was the Christmas of 1942 and not a happy time for a world at war. It was a particularly depressing period for your mother and me, who, along with you and 10,000 other people, were living in a place called Heart Mountain, Wyoming.

This community was made up of row on row of black tar-paper-covered barracks. It was surrounded by barbed wire and guarded by soldiers so we couldn't get out.

We were there because our country, in its infinite ignorance, figured we could not be trusted to be loyal because our forebears had migrated to the United States from Japan. So without bothering to make formal charges, the government suspended our Constitutional rights and forced 115,000 of us Japanese Americans out of our homes and into ten concentration camps in the desert West.

Out of our barracks, we could see only gray sand, scudding gray clouds, gray sagebrush that stretched to the gray horizon. Gray wallboard on four walls and the ceiling of our cubicle, a floor gray with the desert dust ground into the raw plywood.

As Christmas approached, we tried to make our lives brighter with little gifts purchased through mail-order houses, even a little artificial tree fashioned of odds and ends and draped with cotton snow.

Yet the grayness permeated the air, for we were lonely in the midst of the 10,000. It wasn't longing for any particular friends; it was the hollow, numbing feeling of being outcast, unwanted and forgotten. Outcast from the home communities where we belonged, our loyalty suspected by our nation in a war emergency, forgotten by our fellow citizens.

On Christmas Eve, we went to the mess hall for a party. It was crowded with wide-eyed children and their parents trying to be cheerful, and song leaders struggling almost frantically to whip up the Christmas spirit. Slowly the crowd warmed up, joining in singing the carols we had learned as children in a happier time.

Then came Santa Claus, riding from mess hall to mess hall in an olive drab government truck. Clad in an ill-fitting red suit, his whiskers awry, he stomped into our mess hall, full of loud cheer.

The younger children, you among them, gaped in pop-eyed amazement. Many of the tots were too young to remember previous Christmases, and here was a real live Santa Claus with a great bulging sack on his back.

The gifts were passed out, and there was one for everyone, from the youngest child to the oldest grandmother. There were books and toys and games, pictures to hang in bleak barracks, washcloths and toilet soap, trinkets and useful gadgets, all of them poured into the desert camp by the great, generous heart of fellow Americans who had heard of our plight.

Cards from the donors were enclosed with the gifts. They came from the Joneses, the Smiths, and the Browns, and common folk whose names indicated they probably came to America with later waves of immigrants. The gifts were from Billings, Montana, and Boston, Massachusetts; from a mountain town in New Mexico and an orphanage where the youngsters had saved pennies to buy presents for little evacuee children like you who had no homes, either.

The grayness left the camp that night and never really returned. It wasn't due to the presents alone. But they were symbols to remind us that we no longer were forgotten exiles in our native land. They—the American people—remembered us, and had let us know this with an outpouring of affection from cities and hamlets the country over.

I have never forgotten that night, nor the goodness in the hearts of the people who make up our nation.

Nor should you forget that the warmth of America's concern for people in trouble epitomizes the true Christmas spirit.

Have a merry Christmas.

Dad

Epilogue

H. L. Mencken, the iconoclastic writer known as "the Sage of Baltimore," was the darling of a generation of intellectuals and pseudo-intellectuals. They loved his sarcasm and wit, his ability to satirize American conformists, the way he skewered *Boobus americanus* for what he considered stupidity.

Mencken died in 1956, leaving instructions that his diary not be made public for at least twenty-five years. Now, parts of the journal have been published in a book, *The Diary of H. L. Mencken* (Alfred A. Knopf, 1989). What it reveals is not always pretty.

Readers have discovered that Mencken did not like Jews very much (except those he considered friends) and held a condescending view of blacks. These revelations have shocked some of Mencken's admirers, and they would throw stones at his memory.

There are others who say Mencken was the product of his time, that his views were widely shared by his contemporaries, and that a half century ago, it was rare to find anyone who thought about racial prejudice in a way that most fair-minded people do today.

What the latter group is saying is that there is little logic to judging the past—in this case, Mencken's views—by the standards of the present. To dredge up a parallel, take Thomas Jefferson, whose concepts of freedom and justice played a major part in shaping the Constitution. Yet he was a slave owner. He believed in the dignity of man, but he accepted the standards of his time. Should he be condemned as a bigot for this?

There's a word for this human inclination to criticize old-fashioned thinking and actions by holding them up to contemporary measuring sticks, which we now believe reflect the true gospel: *presentism.* I ran across this word—which I didn't know existed—with not a little delight in a recent issue of *Newsweek* magazine. For all its utility and appropriateness, it's probably an expression concocted to meet the needs of the present, because it isn't in my *Webster's Third International Dictionary.*

We make much of presentism in the Japanese American community. Some of us have made a career of looking in rearview mirrors, spending more time searching for and lamenting the terrible things that have already happened than in attending to what is happening today and preparing for what lies ahead.

Much like the call to excommunicate Mencken for voicing the common wisdom of his era is the pastime of applying today's standards to criticize the Nisei decision to comply with federal evacuation orders in wartime 1942. Both the times and our understanding of what is proper have changed. We are in an era of protest, when citizens routinely take to the streets to express feelings about such disparate matters as abortion, gun control, homosexuality, fur coats, tuna fish, whaling, and the spotted owl. The Supreme Court says burning the Stars and Stripes is an acceptable form of free speech. That wasn't true in 1942. Fifty years from now, what will a new generation of presentism advocates say in scorning the attitudes we embrace today?

I'm glad to discover *presentism,* a good word to describe our inability to be logical. I hope we don't have to use it too frequently.

I began writing this book on my antediluvian Apple II computer. I had completed 60 or 70 pages when the computer died, its memory vanishing into the black electronic void from which there is no return. My youngest granddaughter Stephanie Boatright, then in junior high school, rescued my from my desperation. Her parents, Warren and Susan, located a computer wizard who somehow exhumed the electronic impulses and Stephanie inputted them onto a disk my replacement computer could read. That saved the writing project. I am humble and grateful.